T0089818

The Happy Medium

The Happy Medium

Life Lessons from the Other Side

Kim Russo

HARPERELIXIR
An Imprint of HarperCollinsPublishers

This book is metaphysical and philosophical in nature. Nothing herein is intended to imply an endorsement of the book, author, or publisher by any of the persons mentioned herein, including the celebrities and their families. The intent of the author is only to offer information of a general nature to help you in your quest for emotional and spiritual well-being. In the event you use any of the information in this book for yourself, the author and publisher assume no responsibility for your actions.

The individual experiences recounted in this book are true. However, in some instances, names and other descriptive details have been altered to protect the identities of the people involved.

HarperCollins books may be purchased for educational, business, or sales promotional use. For information, please e-mail the Special Markets Department at SPsales@harpercollins.com.

HarperCollins website: http://www.harpercollins.com

FIRST HARPERCOLLINS PAPERBACK EDITION PUBLISHED IN 2017

Designed by Paul Barrett

Library of Congress Cataloging-in-Publication Data is available upon request.

ISBN 978–0–06–245626–7

23 24 25 26 27 LBC 13 12 11 10 9

We cannot teach people anything;
we can only help them discover
it within themselves.

—Galileo

To my heavenly Father the Creator of this vast and wonderful universe: It is your infinite wisdom that teaches me, your strength that sustains me, and your love that nurtures me. Without you, none of this would be possible. It is to you I humbly dedicate this book and give all the glory and praise.

To my team of spirit guides who patiently waited for me to remember the reason I was born and who continue to guide me throughout my life, delivering reassuring signs and clearing the path for me to make a difference: Thank you for assisting me in all of my soul lessons, big and small, and thank you for always knowing what is best for me, especially when I don't.

And to the many departed souls I have met over the years: It is with a humble heart and great honor that I serve as your voice. Thank you for trusting me to deliver countless heartfelt messages to your loved ones. Through them you have made me laugh and you have made me cry, but most of all, you have made me believe that who we really are never dies.

Contents

Introduction

WHAT'S THE FIRST WORD that pops into your head when you think about psychic mediums? It's okay—you can say it. There was a time when I also thought of them as quacks. I imagined that they wore long flowing robes, big hoop earrings, and maybe even turbans. In my mind, they were like those gypsy women who coax you into giving them money to light candles and ward away evil, or to scry into a crystal ball and tell you what your future will hold.

I am not any of those things, of course. I am the mother of three grown sons; a loving wife, married to the same man for twenty-eight years; and until recently, the loyal caregiver of two of the most amazing shih tzu dogs, Mugsy and Maggie, who both lived to the ripe old age of eighteen. When many people meet me, they say I remind them of someone they know. Their BFF Donna, their neighbor Lisa, or even just someone they'd love to hang out with. Occasionally people tell me that I look like Paula Abdul or Kirstie Alley, but never once has anyone said, "Hey, you know—you look like you could be a psychic." I do my own laundry, clean my own home, and cook my own meals. I consider myself to be a very level-headed, grounded, and logical person.

Why am I telling you all of this? Because spiritual gifts aren't granted only to special individuals who sit in the yoga position on faraway mountaintops and chant all day long. They are also given to very ordinary people like you and me. You never know—your favorite teacher, doctor, lawyer, or police officer may possess a keen sense of intuition or any number of other psychic gifts they prefer to keep hidden like a shameful secret.

I kept my abilities under wraps for a long time too. I was an executive secretary for a real estate firm up until the day my husband, Anthony, and I decided to start a family.

Anthony is now retired, but over the years he held as many jobs as he had to for me to be a stay-at-home mom for our three boys. We had always planned for me to go back to work and pick up where I left off once the kids were in school full-time. They are older now and done with their studies, except I definitely did not pick up where I left off. With the encouragement of many sincere and knowing people, I openly acknowledged and pursued my true calling. When I was very young, I fantasized that my calling was to be a professional singer. I loved the idea of standing on stage with a microphone, making people feel happy with what was coming from my voice.

Fast-forward many years later and—though I still love music and I do stand on stage holding a microphone, making people feel happy with what is coming from my voice—it is all very different than I ever imagined. Rather than inspiring crowds with my singing voice, I inspire them with my speaking voice, relaying messages of hope, love, and inspiration from the world beyond. With greater understanding of what psychic mediums can do to enlighten and uplift themselves and others, I have effectively gone from being a reluctant and undercover medium to being, as many people call me, the Happy Medium. I'm able to provide great pleasure to so many people, and myself, doing what I do now.

I'm often asked why some people have this gift while others don't, and my answer always seems to come as a surprise: We all have psychic abilities. Every one of us is born with them. They are part of our spiritual DNA. This gift is about energy and how each of us can use ours best. Science has proved that everything in the universe is made of energy. Essentially, what you will discover in this book is that the energy of the soul has a unique vibratory imprint that is able to transcend time and space. The difference between those who exercise their psychic abilities and those who don't even know they have them lies in developing a better understanding of energy and how our senses—not just our five senses, but our extra ones too—interact with energy to help us know things on a much deeper level.

As a child, I didn't know what any of this meant. I did not understand energy. All I knew was when I was in my bedroom alone, the room was filled with visitors that most people couldn't see. Many of the people I encountered in my everyday life did not understand the science of energy either. I was raised to be a good Christian and was taught that if I loved and trusted God then I had nothing to fear—God and all of his helpers would always be by my side. As it happens, I didn't need to learn this from any church or school because I naturally felt a supreme presence around me from the time I could walk and talk. But some of the same people who were telling me this—authority figures I counted on for validation—were also sending me extremely mixed signals about God's love when it came to the innocent exercise of my extra senses. My heart felt that using all the senses I was born with was right, but the world told me it was wrong.

In my quest to find the truth, I discovered that it does not matter who you are, what you are, or where you came from. It does not matter what religion you were born into or what modality you currently practice. What matters is that we are all a chip off the old block of one Divine Source of life. We were never meant to be separate from the whole. Just as fish cannot survive out of water because they need water to thrive, so do humans absolutely need the energy of this Divine Source to get closer to who we really are.

I will consider myself a student of the Universe for as long as I live. I do not claim to have all the answers regarding the world of the unknown; however, by sharing my journey of discovery with you here, it is my goal to help demystify some of it for you in the simplest way possible.

As you continue to read you will learn how the spirit world ultimately opened the door for me to share my knowledge through television and books, and how what I've discovered along the way affects you too. I hope to encourage you to let go of the limiting fears and beliefs on the subject of life and death that have been passed down to us for generations by our respective families, governments, and religions.

Together we'll explore such questions as *Where do we go when we leave our physical body? Who will we meet when we get there? How can we best communicate with those in these other realms?* And, as the title suggests, *What can we gather from their knowledge to help us achieve greater purpose, peace, understanding, and balance in this life and the next?*

This book is also intended to be a practical guide to seeking, finding, talking to, and learning from Spirit directly. It invites you to engage in greater self-discovery and to recognize and use the power within you to connect more fully with others—with those who have wisdom to share from the great beyond, with your loved ones in the here and now, and with your deepest soul, which has been evolving through many lifetimes to become the person you are at this very moment.

It does not matter where you are on your spiritual quest; my aim in writing this book is to help *everyone*. I hope that it will give you the tools to begin your own remarkable journey, and that as you read my story with an open mind and an open heart, it may even give you the courage to find and begin using your own gifts too. Trust me, there's a divine reason as to why you picked up this book. The spirit world clearly has a message for you, so ready or not, here we go!

—Kim Russo

Part 1

What the Spirit World Is
Dying to Teach You

Chapter 1

Don't I Know You from Somewhere?

How a Past-Life Regression Proved That
the Bonds of Love Survive Physical Death

"HOLD ON, ANTHONY! HOLD ON," I said, trying to calm us both down. My husband was sound asleep, and yet he was gurgling and desperately gasping for air. No, he was not having a bad dream. He was revisiting a former lifetime in which he had died by drowning. He was telling me all about what had happened to him, when suddenly the roiling waters pulled him under again. In that moment I worried that Anthony was in real danger—that if I didn't act fast enough, history might repeat itself. *What made me think I was ready to conduct a past-life regression?*

That's right. Those of you who watch my television show, *The Haunting Of . . .* , know me as a medium, but before I ever ventured to do my first psychic reading, I was into practicing a very different modality. I hypnotized people to help them explore and uncover past-life memories. My loving husband was my test case. Not only is he a very patient and agreeable spouse, but he is also what is known as a *somnambulist*—the perfect candidate for hypnosis because he can reach a deep enough level of sleep where he is capable of retrieving information and answering questions without the influence of the conscious mind. Only 20 percent of the world's population has the natural ability to reach this state. Lucky me!

On the night of that first session with Anthony, as he was struggling to stay afloat, I quickly thumbed through the pages of the library book I was using as a guide for my little experiment. I must have missed some important detail. "What do I do now?" I thought. Thankfully my gaze fell on the answer. As I threw my husband a lifeline according to the book's instructions, I made a mental note: "Next time, tell him to look down and *observe* his past life, not *relive* it. That is, of course, if he grants me a next time."

Fortunately, he did grant me subsequent regressions over the years, and what I discovered during those sessions was that he had lived many, many prior lives. More than one was spent at sea. But before I relay the story of how he was a ship captain and explain its relevance to my understanding and current practice of mediumship, I must tell you that I am and always have been a natural-born skeptic. I am a truly logical person who doesn't believe in things I cannot see, feel, or touch. I don't want to just *know* if something is possible; I always want to know *how* something is possible. Although I'm very well read on the subject, most of what I know about the spirit world was learned by doing, which happens to require a healthy dose of that skepticism and a good deal of curiosity too. My quest is always to break things down to their simplest component, and I do that by asking questions. Lots of them.

One night, while sending Anthony back to a previous lifetime, his answers to my questions truly shocked me. I never gave him any suggestions as to where to go—what time period or what age—because when you lead the mind, its responses are not original. He began, as always, with a rhythmic breathing. That's usually how I know he is in a trance and that he has arrived at his destination. Anyone who does hypnosis will recognize this type of breathing.

I saw his eyes roaming around beneath his lids too. They were retrieving information about his surroundings. My first question, of course, was "Where are you?"

He told me, "I'm in the middle of the ocean."

"What are you doing?"

"We're on the ship."

I noticed he was taking five breaths between answers so I paced my questions accordingly. "Who's steering the ship?"

"I am. I'm the captain."

"Are you on the ship alone?"

"No, I'm with my brother."

At that moment I saw him getting very, very uncomfortable. His forehead furrowed and his eyes squinted as if he was in pain. "What's the matter?" I asked.

His response was weak but audible. "My brother. Very sick. No food, no food. He has a high fever."

"Why does he have a high fever?"

All Anthony kept saying was "No food. No food."

Then I asked, "What's your brother's name?

"William. Billy."

That's when I instructed him to look into Billy's eyes. "Who is Billy? Is Billy in your life today?"

A very surprised look crossed his face. "It's Joseph," he said.

Joseph, by the way, is our middle child.

After getting over my own surprise I asked, "What are you doing?"

"I'm fishing. I have to catch a fish. We have to eat. There's no fish in sight. I have to take care of my brother."

I wondered aloud, "Who's older—him or you?"

"I am. I'm the oldest."

Now this would definitely be the time to tell you that in our present life, Joseph and my husband have never behaved like father and son. They have a wonderful camaraderie. They are truly close. But whenever they would fight I'd have to tell Anthony, "You're his father, not his brother. Why are you arguing with him the way a sibling would?" I'd say the same thing to Joseph. "That's not one of your brothers—that's not Nicholas or Anthony Jr. That's your father. You cannot talk to your father like that." Until this very moment there was no rhyme or reason as to why either of them acted this way with each other. But after that night, it all made perfect sense.

Anthony told me, "Billy's throwing up on the side of the ship." Then he added again, "The fever's bad." Just as he shared this information I heard Joseph call out to me from the hallway outside our master bedroom.

"Mommy, I feel sick," he said. Standing at the threshold of our door, he vomited right then and there. I hopped out of bed, leaving Anthony still in his past life. I grabbed a towel and ran to my son. Joseph was burning hot. He had a temperature of 101. I cleaned him up, gave him some aspirin, and walked him back to his room. I still don't really understand what happened that night. Did Joseph go back to this same life Anthony was revisiting? Was he just so in tune with Anthony that he naturally gravitated there too? Or is this evidence of the theory that we live in parallel universes where all of life—past, present, and future is happening at the same time? I have no idea. But this much I do know—*we share a much deeper connection with many of the people in our lives today than we realize. And this connection clearly transcends time and space.*

As a side note, the very next morning Joseph showed no signs of fever or sickness whatsoever. He ate a hearty breakfast and was fine—completely fine. No virus. Nothing. Why am I telling you all of this in the very first chapter of my book?

Well, for a couple of reasons.

First, because I think it proves right up front that mine has *not* been an ordinary life. How many people do you know who've been driven to hypnotize their husband to help satisfy a compulsive curiosity about the mysteries of life and death—a curiosity that began at age nine after a chance encounter with ghosts and continues to this day with thousands more spirits occupying my space?

But it's also here to illustrate where "Let them lead you"—my personal mantra, and the mantra of this book—comes from. As I've said publicly many times before, I never asked for this life, but I firmly believe this life chose me. Yes, I've asked countless questions that have gotten me deeper and deeper into this pursuit, but who wouldn't under the same circumstances? The point is I've always known that there is another place we all come from and that what we presently see is not all there is. My team of spirit guides knows everything about how I think and how I process things. And one thing they knew for sure was that in order to get me on board with my mission, they would have to give me hard-core evidence of this invisible world that most of us cannot see—this invisible world I was to become an interpreter for. I wouldn't have the understanding of life that I do today—a small part of which I just shared with you now—without their incredible resourcefulness and guidance. So with an open mind, let's backtrack together to the start of my story and allow the events and what I took away from each of them to lead you to a greater understanding too. Remember, when the student is ready, the teacher will appear. I promise you it's going to be a wild and fun ride.

Chapter 2

Nightmare on Eighty-Sixth Street

Learning to Overcome Fear

DAYTIME IN MY EARLY childhood home was as idyllic as it gets. My close-knit Italian family enjoyed good food, laughter, and most of all, one another's company. My father came from humble roots. He was an immigrant from Naples, Italy, who lived through the potato famine. As a result he was a hard worker who was grateful for everything he had. When he and his sister Pasqualina, whom we all call Aunt Patti, came to the United States, Patti and my mom became fast friends. My mother is first-generation Italian-American, so she helped my aunt get acclimated. She taught Patti English, and Patti helped improve my mom's Italian.

It was through Patti that my parents met and ultimately fell in love. In time my dad and mom married. They always wanted a big family and were thrilled to raise me and my siblings, John, Sue, and Neil. When we outgrew the small cottage we were living in behind my grandparents' house in Ozone Park, New York, some property right around the corner became available that was big enough to build two adjoining three-family houses on. After the homes were completed, we moved into one while Aunt Patti and her family moved into the other. With that many loved ones around there was never a dull moment. In addition to my siblings, I would always play with my cousins Mary, Carmela, and Anthony. We had endless hours of fun together all year round. During the summer we'd swim in the pool out back and eat al fresco, enjoying the delicious meals my mother and aunt prepared together. During the winter we enjoyed ice-skating in our very own homemade rink, and drinking huge mugs of hot chocolate until we were warm enough to feel our toes again. And if I ever needed to get away from all the activity, my bedroom provided the perfect sanctuary. It was located in the back of the house and was big enough to share with Sue. I'd go there to read or have long conversations with my friends Jesus and Mary. Although Ozone Park had public schools, my parents sent us to a Catholic school around the block from our home. Here is where I first learned that God loves me sooo much . . . as long as I followed a long laundry list of dos and don'ts. I often wondered, "What if I crossed that line? Would God still love me?" Those burning questions seemed to set the tone for many struggles I later had to overcome. But in the meantime, I loved learning about Jesus and his mother, Mary, and forming an immediate bond with their loving energy. I was always so infatuated with them. While I knew they were real, their magical powers made them seem like fictional characters in a great novel to me. I felt unusually close to them, or I should say, I felt they were close to me. I loved the time I spent in that room with them. I could always find peace there while the sun was still shining.

Nights in that bedroom, though, were very different. You could say they were just as *spirited* as they were when I was an adult staying up till dawn talking to the entities Anthony brought through to me. But it was different as a kid. I was terrified then.

The room was actually fairly well lit even at night because of the street lamp outside. From our window I could see the faint outline of the church across the way, and on Sunday mornings I would wake to the sound of its bells. But even those consolations never made me feel safe enough after sundown.

Long before I had my first glimpse of ghosts, I insisted that my sister's and my twin beds be pushed together so we could sleep side by side in the equivalent of a king-size bed. I also claimed the position closest to the door, although I wasn't really sure why until the night they first arrived. There were five spirits in total. The men wore black suits and the women wore drab black dresses. I didn't know the words "immigrant attire" back then, but if I had, that is how I would have described their clothes. Their faces were very austere. They never once cracked a smile, nodded, or even tried to speak to me. Yet their persistent appearance night after night let me know they wanted my attention. One of the women held her palms up in a gesture that suggested she was carrying a plate or box, though no object was ever visible in her hands. Was it an offering? Or was she asking me for something? I never quite knew. Most children look for a sign from adults that lets them know they are safe in their presence—some small hint, a facial expression or body movement that gives them permission to interact. But those signs never came, so I remained uneasy and frightened.

Although Sue is not much older than I am, she is the best big sister a girl could have. She has a very nurturing spirit and has always looked out for me. As enormous as our childhood bed was, I always ended up nestled close to her. I still apologize for having kept her up so late. We laugh about it now, but back in those days it wasn't so funny. To make sure she wouldn't fall asleep and leave me to contend with the apparitions alone, I would tell her all about my day at school, recounting bits of information I learned and spelling new words aloud. One night I tried to prolong the inevitable by picking the longest word I could think of and then I sounded it out for her. E-L-E-P-H-A-N-T. When I was done, the spirits appeared at the foot of the bed, clear as day. I couldn't take it anymore. Sue had begun to doze off, but I shook her.

"Sue, Sue, Sue," I cried.

"What? What?" she said, rousing only slightly.

"Look over there! Right at the corner of the bed. In the light. Look, look!"

Despite my shouting, the spirits didn't even budge.

"Do you see them? Do you see those people?" I asked.

"I don't see anything."

"They're right there, right there. You don't see them?"

At that point I was holding Sue's arm so tightly I'm sure I stopped her circulation.

"Kim, I don't see anything."

At first I thought my sister was playing a joke on me. She had to see them. But whether she did or she didn't, I'm the type of person who knows what I know and I never doubt myself. And besides, at least the cat was out of the bag now. Sue finally knew about the ghosts in the night, and now that she knew, I had a confidante. As time went on I'd tell her, "Sue, these people, they're coming a lot more now. They have me staying up all night. They follow me to school too. I can feel them breathing down my neck." Her advice most times was "Just close your eyes and tell them to go away." She'd also tell me to pray the Our Father, which I did. We had these beautiful wooden rosary beads that had been blessed by the pope hanging over our bed, so I'd say all the Hail Marys too. But I still felt the spirits. Closing my eyes might have blocked these souls from my view but there was no avoiding their stare. It would burn a hole right through me.

Even if my sister didn't see ghosts, she never made me feel like I was crazy. In fact, one night when we returned home from visiting cousins in Long Island, I saw a light in the hallway by the entrance to the room that clearly wasn't from the street lamp. I begged my father to go in before us and check under the bed and in the closet. Sue told my dad she thought somebody was in the room too. I felt a seriousness in her voice, so I knew she wasn't just saying it to appease me. I looked at her and I said, "But you told me you don't see them." I'm grateful for her answer to this day: "No, but I know they're there. I just didn't want you to be more scared than you already are."

The coast was clear that night, and I went to bed with the added peace and assurance that someone believed me. Many years later, my cousin rented the same space in my parents' house where I had lived until we moved to Long Island. His young daughters reported seeing the very same spirits, in the very same bedroom. I wish they had relayed this to me earlier than they did. I probably could have saved them many sleepless nights. Or could I have?

WHAT'S UP WITH GHOSTS AND KIDS?

I learned firsthand when I was a child, and of course when I explored this phenomenon as an adult, that one of the primary reasons ghosts frequently appear to kids is because kids naturally have an open heart. What I mean by that is the world is so new to children, their curiosity leads them to use *all* of their senses to experience it. In addition to their five senses (sound, sight, touch, smell, and taste), which are ruled by what we call the *ego mind,* they also actively use their sixth sense (their collective emotions, feelings, and intuition), which is ruled by their heart. There are many influences in culture that ultimately cause us to develop and use our ego mind more than our heart, so in time most people experience the world using their sixth sense far less than we all have the capacity to.

Some children, however, never lose touch with their heart center. They are called *empaths*—deriving from the word *empathy*—because when a person feels emotions from their heart and not just from their head, a form of compassion we know as empathy easily follows.

For instance, I was an empathic child, which meant I not only felt my own feelings and those of the people geographically close to me, but also felt (and still feel) what was going on with people I love living far away, such as my aunts and uncles and now my mother and youngest son. Empaths can even transcend time and space to connect with energies that are in another dimension. Oddly enough, I think this happened with those very first ghosts I saw. When I was in my late teens, my mother showed me pictures of relatives in an old family photo album she kept. I was shocked to see people among them I recognized. Some of them looked exactly like the spirits I saw every single night of my childhood. There was no mistake about it. I had seen those spirits so often I could sketch their faces detail for detail. One guy had these unforgettably bony, hollow cheeks. He looked like he could use a good meal. And in addition to all of their familiar faces was the very specific clothing they wore—garments right out of the Depression era, just like what many immigrants wore when they came to this country. Although these relatives remained behind in Italy, they may have been attached to our home because my dad was very involved in its construction. He had hands of gold. He was a house painter by trade, but there was nothing he couldn't build or fix. He made his mark, and then some, after leaving his country and coming to this land of opportunity where he made a great life for us.

To help you understand how connecting with these spirits was even possible, let me give you a little crash course in energy.

The energy that empathic people are in touch with is very real. We each draw it from the Source of all things. Actually, whether we are empathic or not, all of us have seven main centers inside of us that channel and conduct this energy throughout our body. These centers are called *chakras*. They are positioned between the crown of our head and the base of our spine. Because energy is constantly in motion, it emits *vibrations* or *frequencies*. As a result, everyone and everything is surrounded by an energy field known as an *aura*. It is this aura, or more specifically the energy frequencies the aura contains, that empaths detect. Since ghosts—or earthbound souls, as I prefer to call them— are made entirely of energy that is no longer shrouded in a body, highly sensitive children are able to feel and intuit their presence. Even before I was able to see the ghosts in my childhood bedroom, I had a feeling they were there because I picked up on their vibrations. In time I used my heart sense to help visualize them too.

By the way, the fact that all things, including souls, are made of energy is what makes those of us who study souls so sure they can live many lives. Energy, as we know from the example of water, can be transmuted into different forms. Water begins as a liquid, but when frozen it becomes a solid, or when heated it becomes a vapor, proving that energy can be recycled but not destroyed. So it is with the soul.

WHAT PREVENTS SO MANY OTHER PEOPLE FROM DETECTING THESE ENERGIES?

I used to ask myself this question every time I thought about how no one else but me could see the sprits that were clearly right in front of us. The answer took a long time to process and has everything to do with a number of institutional barriers society puts in our way.

Starting from the time we come into this world, our parents' influence has us seeing everything through their eyes. We are conditioned to believe what they believe. Their values become our values.

Then we enter school and are forced to embrace and accept what is being taught in our classrooms. For most kids, the day they enter kindergarten is when the balance between their five senses and that mysterious sixth sense shifts. That is when the ego mind begins to take precedence. You enter a classroom full of strangers and what do you notice? Most kids check out everyone else's clothes and, later, the contents of their lunch box. They pretty quickly get a sense of who's popular with the teacher and who's even more popular with other kids. That's when the comparisons and consequently the emotional separation from others starts. The first time we feel "all alone" or "not good enough" is the moment our connections to others' feelings and energies become less noticeable to us than our own.

As we grow older, there is the matter of grades, rankings, and acceptance into advanced studies, specialized high schools, colleges, and universities. What is emphasized is memorization and fact-based knowledge that can be uniformly tested so we can all graduate and be labeled as *qualified to work*. But this only distances us further from the empathy we naturally had as kids.

Drilling information into us also minimizes the development of other kinds of knowing. I'd really love to see a day when psychic abilities become a part of our educational curriculum the way health, science, or history is. Studies have shown that empathy is a vital life skill that helps determine our success even more than a high IQ does. I like to think I'm smart, but being able to connect with others' feelings even when I'm not conducting a psychic reading is what has led me to where I am today—and a lot faster than if I operated on my own. But until the time that our EQ (emotional quotient) is as valued as our intelligence quotient in places such as school or work, we're not likely to fully understand the energy that is all around us—energy that includes our various spirit guides, angels, and loved ones who have gone into the light, as well as those spirits who are lagging behind on earth. Energy that also includes the positive and negative thoughts, feelings, and emotions of the people we come in contact with every day.

The institution of religion also throws us a curveball. The great irony here is that while religion is designed to connect us with the source of all energy, it can often separate us from vital energies too. This is done through the barrier of fear. From early on in my religion class, I heard the wonderful news that our souls are everlasting, but somehow after we leave earth, our souls become off-limits to the living. We are instilled with the notion that the dead have a DO NOT DISTURB sign on their door. But for me, it was the other way around. *What's a girl to do when these souls have a different set of rules and come knocking on her door?* I cringe whenever I think about how many passages exist in Scripture warning us against talking to the dead in any way. The mere mention of them used to put the fear of God in me because whether I liked it or not, spirits were around me, eager to communicate, all the time. I wondered if the Catholic Church was right. Could it be that some spirits are actually evil forces preying on our goodness? Could they really be the devil out to ensnare and tempt me into sin? If so, how do I tell the good ones from the bad?

What kept me sane and faithful, though, was the discovery of other passages that addressed the importance of this interaction, as you will read about in chapter 4.

The movie industry is also a notorious culprit in spreading fear, for sure. Scary movies and TV shows aren't just released at Halloween. They seem to never end. There are spin-offs and whole franchises multiplying too quickly to count, with so many of these stories portraying ghosts as nightmare-inducing ghouls. Yes, the trapped souls who stood at the foot of my bed throughout my early childhood were terrifying, but not because they wanted to eat my soul, crush my skull, or shame me into admitting what I did last summer. They were terrifying because I hadn't yet developed the means to truly converse with them. I didn't understand their plight, so I had no way of knowing what they wanted from me or what I could do to help them.

Now I know you aren't shocked to learn that Hollywood perpetuates fear, but did you ever think about the subtle role most parents play in this too? After Mom and Dad let their children watch these movies, they send them to bed with one very false and not particularly reassuring message: "Don't worry, kids. Ghosts aren't real." From a very early age, children constantly check in with their parents for guidance and approval. As is true with any relationship that is newly forming, the bonding process occurs when both parties seem to have a mutual agreement. You can't imagine what empathic kids are left to feel when they experience the energy of something they've been told doesn't exist—especially when it's a loved one who has duped them. You guessed it. They are overcome with a heart-wrenching, paralyzing fear that isolates and segregates them from others.

Many of the myths society has created cause such anxiety that we soon believe some doors to understanding are better left closed. But I've always been a big believer in shining a light to make a dark room less daunting.

To put it simply, we are a product of what we have learned—we are the result of all the thoughts, fears, views, and age-old practices our family and other societal influences have downloaded into our consciousness. But just like a computer, your thoughts can be reprogrammed and you can unlearn what does not work for you—it's never too late. Just saying.

To help you determine if you were empathic at a young age, if you still are today, or if your child is, I've included a quick test at the end of this chapter. As you answer its questions, remember that *all* of us have the capacity to see and interact with energy until society conditions us not to. It is very much like singing. Just about everyone can do it. Very few of us will have a voice as strong as Barbra Streisand's, but the vast majority of us can at least carry a tune. When we are kids we don't hesitate to sing loudly and proudly wherever we are. As adults we restrain ourselves more, limiting our singing mostly to the shower. But imagine what would happen if we all developed that innate skill to the best of our ability?

For those who discover that you have children on that path already, bear in mind, it is crucial they are believed when they confide their experiences in you or others. Be open to helping them by fully exploring what's happening. Ending the cycle of fear really does begin with you. It has been said that FEAR stands for False Expectations Appearing Real and that EGO stands for Edging God Out. Putting in perspective fear and the ego mind really is the first step in developing greater empathy and awakening the dormant sixth sense in us all.

Meditations That Help Nurture Empathy

If you have an empathic child, I have found it's helpful to explain to them that energy is very real and that although we cannot see it, it certainly exists. Teach them what you have just learned about the human aura so they can begin to understand how to read and understand vibrations. Let them know that thoughts—positive or negative—are a form of energy too and can manifest into reality, so they should wish for only positive things. Encourage them to take a moment out of their day to reflect on and be grateful for the good things that happened as a result of their positive vibrations.

If your child feels uneasy about the energy around them and they are not sure why, teach them to visualize an energetic barrier around their own aura. This will protect them from any negative outside influences.

My favorite technique is called the *Bubble Meditation*. Have them close their eyes and visualize a bubble of white light from God, descending from the heavens, reaching all the way down around their feet, encasing them in an egg-shaped sphere of protective light with no holes, rips, or tears. If your child is too young to do this exercise, do it for them. I recommend practicing this a minimum of three times a day. This impression of white protective light will take root immediately, but the more you do it, the more effective it will be. It might also help to have your child think about the tools and powers their favorite superheroes use in combat. Suggest that they imagine themselves using these same shields and superpowers to keep negative forces away. I used this technique with my own children, who were fans of the Power Rangers and other similar characters when they were young.

If you were an empathic child and believe that your heart is still very open at this time, there is an easy meditation I use to teach my students how to raise their vibrations. It is called the *Elevator Meditation*. Simply imagine yourself inside an elevator with no doors so that you are free to step out at any time. As you step inside the elevator you will notice there are many floors you can go up to. Push whatever level you are comfortable with and picture yourself rising to that level, one floor at a time. When you get to a level you like, just stay there and feel what it's like to have your vibrations raised. There you may start to feel others are joining you—perhaps a deceased relative or pet, or maybe your spirit guide. In this moment it is best to let the experience unfold without any expectations. Be the observer rather than the thinker.

IS ANYONE ELSE LIKE ME?

Children whose abilities are well developed at a young age are usually not the only ones in their family with these skills. It might be comforting for them to talk to relatives and compare notes, so don't be shy about bringing up the topic at your family gatherings. You may be surprised at what you discover. As it so happens I have family members who are sensitive to the spirit world too. Many of them are on my father's side. As I mentioned earlier, he and his sisters grew up very poor in Italy before coming to America. All of the children in his family shared a bedroom. They slept on the floor, tucked into sleeping bags made from blankets, sheets, and any other material they could find that might keep them warm. On a nightly basis, they would all observe their sister Irene rise up as if she were in a trance and begin walk-ing around. She'd lift her arms toward the sky and say, *"Vien, angela, vien, angela,"* which in Italian means "Come to me, angels, come to me, angels." While in this trance she would make circular gestures with her hands as if she were greeting these angels upon their arrival. My father said he and his other siblings instinctively knew they were never to wake or interrupt her when this was happening. I remember meeting Aunt Irene for the first time and being taken by the intensity and color of her eyes. They are a deep green—not dark green but more like the color of ripe grapes. They are strikingly, mesmerizingly beautiful and look very much like the eyes in a picture of Jesus I have. She grew up to possess amazing healing powers. I have seen these powers firsthand, as I will detail in subsequent chapters.

My cousin Carmela is highly intuitive too, and though she doesn't practice professionally, she certainly could. But it's the sensitivity of my cousin Mary that is most unusual. When Mary would go to church on Sundays, she would always faint. It was a weekly occurrence and yet nobody made a big deal about it. The priest explained that the pres-ence of the Holy Spirit was so overwhelming for her it would cause her to pass out. He said this was not uncommon in the special healing or charismatic masses practiced in Catholic churches. Apparently a lot of people would just fall to the ground during these events when they could no longer sustain the energy around them. Often the priests would cover them with a cloth until they could recover. They would refer to people fainting with the phrase "getting slain in the Spirit." Mary told us that the Blessed Mother would always come to her before she would faint. When the intensity of Mary's experience subsided, she would just get up, return to the pew, and listen to the rest of the sermon, completely unscathed.

All of this may sound very bizarre to you, and that is the point of me telling you about it. Because for us, it wasn't odd at all. My parents didn't make a fuss one way or another about my sensitivities or about those of other members of the family. It was just generally accepted that the people around me were very attuned to energy. It clearly didn't stop us from having great fun together and creating fabulous memories. I truly remember us being ordinary kids in every other way. Maybe most of your relatives remember only hearing creaks in the attic or seeing lights flash on or off in the house, but I can guarantee that those of you who are more attuned to energy have family members who are too. Someone else besides you has felt chilly bumps for no apparent reason.

A SIGN FROM THE STARS

As proof that so many of us connect with energies outside of our own when we are kids, just look at how many of the guests on *The Haunting Of . . .* revealed incidents from their childhood. Dot Jones and Richard Burgi clearly had psychic abilities since the time they were children. So did Patrick Muldoon and Christopher McDonald, among others. Thankfully these guests never fully sublimated their abilities. They are still on the surface waiting to be recalled. Early in her episode Dot admitted that she has felt energies around her from the time she was young. Even when she is home by herself now, she is aware that she is never truly alone. Then, of course, she went on to read me with a degree of accuracy that was uncanny. Dot and I have remained in touch since the taping of the show, so I know that she has been working hard on taking what was natural to her as a kid and applying it to her present life. I know too that she would tell you it's wonderful to reawaken your connection to energy.

I was so sure Richard had these abilities that I hid an object outside the house where we were meeting before he arrived. I was convinced he would be able to visualize that object for me later. Richard had several brushes with Spirit as a child, which he shared in great detail with me. As I told him then what I often tell people with similar experiences: spirits only appear to those they know can see them. It is interesting that Richard's sister Susie and deceased dad also encountered these energies, which only further validates the notion that these abilities run in families. The spirit of Richard's dad, who came too and guided us during much of the day, said these abilities have run deep within the family for generations. I have no doubt that if Richard and Susie talk with others in the latest generation of Burgis they will discover more empaths just like them. Doesn't it make sense to share these legacies rather than keep them secret? Doing so can allay so many fears, refute so many fallacies . . . and reveal so many latent powers within us in the process!

How Psychic Is Your Child? And How Psychic Were *You* as a Kid?

If you believe you have an empathic child, asking yourself the following questions can help you be sure. If you believe that *you* were empathic as a kid, adapting and answering these questions can also help determine the psychic potential you still have now.

1. *Does your child (or did you) typically avoid large crowds?* Empaths are so sensitive to the energy around them they will often become overwhelmed by lots of activity, noise, or commotion. Overcrowded classrooms, hallways, playgrounds, restaurants, stores, or streets can cause intense bouts of shyness until your child is back in the comfort of his or her own home again.

2. *Does your child act out physically or emotionally when in busy places despite having a calm demeanor at home?* Although this is a different reaction to the same situation described earlier, it is also an example of how

some empaths will respond to the overwhelming flow of incoming energy they are experiencing.

3. *Does your child resist going to bed on time? Does he constantly wake up in the middle of the night? Does he frequently climb into bed with you?* These are signs that he may be trying to find a secure place to center or ground himself in.

4. *Does your child have a low immune system? Does she catch infections easily, especially ear infections?* While not every empath experiences this, it is often a way for some to withdraw from society for a period of time to regroup and filter out any unwanted emotions, especially the uncomfortable ones she may be feeling. The conscious mind doesn't do this purposely, but the subconscious mind does.

5. *Is your child very attracted to people who need help? Is he a nature or animal lover?* Very often empaths are drawn to the "Oneness" or "Wholeness" of the Universe. Most love to be outdoors, even in the cold winter months! And most are passionate about rescuing stray dogs and cats. Even having a fish can bring great comfort to an empathic child. If this is true of your child, be prepared to have an elaborate funeral for Mr. Fish if God forbid anything happens to him. Helping your sensitive child grieve sufficiently is very important to keeping his heart open.

6. *Is your child the peacemaker among her siblings, classmates, or friends?* Empaths have very affectionate, compassionate personalities and will frequently grow up to be of service to others, putting their own needs and wants second to others'.

7. *Is your child subject to major mood swings that leave him or others around him walking on eggshells?* When the feelings of those in their path are too overwhelming or confusing for them, empathic children can have dramatic mood swings. Especially when empaths reveal their abilities to others and don't feel understood or supported, they can learn to suppress their skills, or worse—they can begin to bottle up emotions, both their own and those they absorbed from others. Sadly this can sometimes result in physical and/or emotional illness. Children who experience such mood swings should definitely practice the Bubble Meditation I detailed earlier, and again, if they are too young to do it on their own, do it for them until they can learn to do it for themselves.

Hmm, why do I suspect that most of you and your children have some empathic and psychic tendencies? Even answering yes to just one of these questions means there are potential empathic and psychic abilities to be developed.

Chapter 3

Not a Ghost of a Chance

> *Frequently Haunted Places to Avoid Until You Are an Expert*

JUST ABOUT THE TIME I entered third grade my parents bought a big, beautiful colonial house on two acres in Commack, Long Island. It was like a palace to me. It had really spacious bedrooms, plush carpeting, and grass in the front yard. Nana moved in with us too, but sadly my cousins and best friends Carmela and Mary, who lived next door to us for all those years, stayed in Ozone Park.

Long Island is different from the borough of Queens where our old home was located. It felt as if we were out in the country. You don't just go down the street and hang out with all the other kids who happen to be there; you have to arrange play dates. Sue was older now and off doing her own thing, so I was very lonely at first. But make no mistake about it: I was never *really* alone.

I spent my time in this beautiful room my parents created for my sister and me. It was much larger than the old one we shared. And now we each had *big-girl* beds. Hers was so far from mine it felt as if the place were all my own. It was the first time I'd slept by myself since I was in a crib.

My dad painted the walls bubble-gum pink, and both of my parents made an extra effort to decorate the room so it was fit for a princess. I'm sure they thought making it pretty like that would help us get a better night's sleep. It was so nice—we even had play space for all of our toys and Barbie dolls. But there was a trade-off. Everything might have been grander, but the energy wasn't any better. All that extra space just meant more room for unwanted visitors.

Now there were ten million spirits around me all the time. It was a regular fearfest for me, though these ghosts were different from the ones in the old house. They were more random. I intuitively knew they were never part of the same group because new ones would come and go all the time. Sometimes they would leave me be. Other times they were so close I could feel them breathing down my neck.

I would still always invite Mary and Jesus to come talk with me. I thought, "Well, okay, Jesus is here with me, and Mary is here too, so no one can really hurt me." While the spirits never went away when I did that, praying always gave me peace and helped me feel safe.

To make the move from Queens to Long Island, my dad rented a big moving truck and used his work van to transport all of us and the countless boxes we packed. Some of those boxes carted fragile items and family heirlooms. But you'll never believe who else hitched a ride to the new place. That's right—the immigrant ghosts from Ozone Park! They showed up many nights during those first few weeks when I was treating the move like I was on some kind of vacation that would be over soon.

I know. You're shocked. I was too. Of course, I didn't realize that I had drawn them to me until much later in life when I grew to understand the paranormal world better. I think they had become so much a part of my nightly routine that I looked for them before I went to sleep. Having them there preserved the status quo, at least until I could make the adjustment to my new life.

Then one day the doorbell rang. I was upstairs in my room when my mom called up to say I had company. "Me? Company?" I thought. "How could I have company?" I didn't know anyone. I hadn't even started school yet, as it was still summertime.

My guest turned out to be a girl my age with an adorable, warm smile. She was super friendly and bubbly. "Hi there. I'm Rose," she said. "Welcome to the neighborhood."

Even though she had only just introduced herself, she didn't feel at all like a stranger to me. There was something in her eyes that sparked a memory of a time we spent together before. It was as if we were picking up where we once left off. We clicked immediately, and just like that I had a new best friend. The two of us were inseparable. We were like Frick and Frack. You never saw Kim without Rose and you never saw Rose without Kim. I have pictures—we almost started to look alike. The amazing thing is that in every town I ever moved to, the Universe always provided at least one great friend for me.

Rose had a fabulous fashion sense. Her mother was a seamstress and made all of her daughter's clothes. Needless to say I was impressed. I had had to wear a uniform every day when I was in Catholic school, but now I could wear bell-bottom jeans, marshmallow shoes, and Huk-A-Poo shirts. I was becoming more "myself"—more independent and confident every day. While I never really told anybody other than my sister about my *big* secret, or about Mary and Jesus, I somehow knew Rose would never judge me if I did. Still, I decided to keep the truth to myself—to act as if I were in the witness protection program and I was starting a brand-new life.

My new confidence would serve me well in the months to come. As it turned out, my room wasn't the only place in our new house with over-the-top, megawatt activity. Nana's room was gigantic. We called it the queen's room. She had an en suite bathroom with a full shower and tub, and she had this great king-size bed. She also had the biggest walk-in closet you've ever seen in your life. But it was weird—at the end of this huge closet was a hatched door that led to an attic on the same floor. We'd all scramble to sleep in Nana's room when she went on overnights until we too heard the noises she complained about. The activity in that room was tenfold the activity in my room. I'm not kidding. I heard not only feet stomping in that closet but banging like someone was taking a hammer to the walls. Then there was the constant slamming of doors too.

Now you have to know there is a thin line between being curious and being a wacko, and I pretty much crossed that line—I don't think any other kid would go back into that room after what I heard. But I just had to investigate. I was born to be a detective.

Whenever there were noises, I'd quickly run and get my mother. Once she came in, the clamor would always stop. When she would leave, it would start up again. I felt like this entity had a heartbeat and intelligence. It had a personality, but I didn't feel that it was friendly. It enjoyed playing tricks on me too much. I didn't back down, though. I started to talk to it, but always in my head. I never spoke aloud to it. I even went into the closet to try to coax it out of hiding. I'd mentally tell it, "Whoever you are, I want to see you. Reveal yourself." I mean, I had brass ones. I knew I wouldn't be that frightened if it showed itself because I had seen spirits my whole childhood. I just wanted to know who it was that was trying to antagonize us.

And these weren't the only disturbances. There was a terrible grease fire in our kitchen that did tremendous damage. It still amazes me that our whole house didn't burn down during the incident. There were also ongoing arguments in our home that never seemed to occur before. You could cut the tension with a knife. My dad was working long hours and was rarely home due to his extended commute. He was exhausted all the time and my mother worried that he was wearing himself thin. And if that wasn't challenging enough, there was what we all refer to as "the plague." No one knows how it happened, but we each contracted an awful staph infection that lasted for a year. One by one, we began breaking out with huge boils on our skin that were so painful we couldn't endure even the slightest touch. My mother had to constantly do laundry in scalding water to kill any residual germs that may have oozed onto our clothes or bedsheets. We each had designated towels and our garments couldn't be thrown into the same hamper. The abscesses multiplied faster than any of them could possibly heal. My dad had one on his elbow that was so big that when it was finally drained you could see straight through to the bone. Forgive me for being so graphic, but when I say it was like the plague, I really mean it. Thankfully none of the visitors to our home during that time caught it—not even our closest friends, though the doctors warned us that it was highly contagious. It was a blessing that they didn't, but you have to admit it's also a bit odd.

I won't even get into how traumatized I was by a bully in my class who punched me in the stomach every day for a year or how my sister narrowly escaped being abducted by a man with a gold tooth who followed her after school one day and tried to lure her into his car. She kicked him where the sun don't shine and ran like crazy. Although she thought she lost him, she saw him again on the afternoon we moved from that horrible house. He was parked behind the moving truck and winked at her when she passed by. How scary to think that he knew where we lived all along. I truly believe her angels were working overtime to keep her safe. All of our angels were.

Now I'm not saying some of these things wouldn't have happened in another house, but all of us had the same uneasy thoughts. My mother was the first to verbalize it. She said that ever since we moved into that house everything changed. Nothing was the same. Bad things were happening, and when I heard her fears, I agreed. I didn't believe it because she said it; I believed it because it made sense to me and it was true. She was the one to point it out, though.

When we started doing research on the house, we discovered all kinds of stories about the people who'd died there. An old lady passed away in the home, and a young man was killed in a motorcycle accident right on the corner. Then, of course, we heard lots of talk about the place right next door to ours. It was the creepiest-looking home I'd ever seen. Apparently it was built in the early 1800s by a very wealthy family. The property belonging to this family stretched over 350 acres, which meant that the land our home was built on was initially theirs. At one time a family-owned hotel was located on the property to help house the countless visitors these business owners entertained. As was customary at the time, a family cemetery was also located on the grounds. Because the energies of so many different kinds of people and spirits linger in both hotels and cemeteries, we wondered if the occurrences we were experiencing could have possibly been coming from that mansion. But in the back of my mind, I also wondered if all this supernatural activity happened because of me. Did I stir up this stuff? Whatever it was, it definitely contributed to our decision to move from there a few years later.

While I now visit places filled with spirits all the time in order to help people understand the meaning of their hauntings, I left that home in Commack with more questions than answers. What I wanted to know was why spirits get trapped, which ones are generally safe, and which ones I should avoid. I wanted to know all the potential places these spirits could inhabit and if my home was an anomaly or if there were other hotbeds of activity that attracted as many souls at once. And this is what, after thousands of conversations with Spirit, I have found out:

WHY DO SOME SPIRITS STAY TRAPPED IN THIS PHYSICAL DIMENSION?

After a body dies, the soul typically moves toward the "light of the whole," also referred to as the "light of the God force." The reasons some souls do not move in this direction run the gamut from the very basic to the extremely complex.

Some souls are actually stunned at the time of their death. They may have been victims of violence or they may have had a traumatic accident. In any event, their death was unexpected and the confusion that followed derailed them. They may not even realize or accept that they are dead. In unanticipated deaths, the souls may even feel as if they were taken too soon or that they still have a lot left to do. Of course, not every soul who died suddenly and without warning is trapped. The vast majority move on safely into the light.

Some souls remain because they are still attached to people, pets, places, or possessions that are here. They may believe that no one else will care for these loved ones or belongings as well as they did. Some may have been control freaks when they were alive in the physical body, as most souls keep their personalities intact once they leave the earth.

Other souls stay behind because of fear. They have no idea what awaits them on the other side. Death is a total mystery to them. That is why books that so openly explore death and the afterlife, such as this one, are so important.

Some souls remain because they still want to be heard, to have a platform, to have a voice. Many have unresolved issues they wish to address before moving on.

Still others, whose passing was self-inflicted, may stay behind because of regret. Again, this is *not* true of all souls who committed suicide, accidentally overdosed on drugs, or drank themselves to death. If you have lost a loved one in this way, take heart. Not every soul who dies in the same way travels the same path in the afterlife. Most who take their own life make it safely to the other side where their actions are viewed with compassion and understanding for the complexities of the emotional distress and mental illness they may have suffered. And those souls who do get trapped after being responsible for their own death will often find redemption helping others who are in the same predicament they once were in to choose life instead of self-destruction. The assistance they lend to troubled people in the here and now earns them increased vibrations when they do ultimately return to the light.

HOW DO YOU KNOW IF THE GHOSTS AROUND YOU ARE SAFE OR NOT?

To my mind there are confused souls, attached souls, mischievous souls, and malevolent souls. I won't comment on demonic souls because I don't and won't travel in their circles.

Confused souls are usually harmless. They are yearning for help. They appeal to those they are sure can see them. Remember what I said earlier about why kids see ghosts more often than adults do. These spirits seek people with open hearts. They are floundering, looking for direction. Many times they are still in the same mind-set as when they died. Whatever reality they were in then seems very real and important to them now. They are hoping you can shed some light on their situation and help them find their way again. Because some of them are not even aware that they have passed, they may continue to do the kinds of work they have always done. There is no sense of time or space in their dimension, so they can engage in repetitive acts without any awareness that they did the same thing moments or days ago in our dimension. Sometimes that is what those odd sounds you hear around your home or the electrical problems you experience are all about. These spirits' constant activity can be maddening to us, but to them it's like Groundhog Day all over again. If you can put your fear aside, you can help these souls continue their journey into the light.

Attached souls are a mixed bag. On the more positive side, some souls connect with you because you remind them of a loved one they've lost. They often use their love to guide and protect you.

Other attached souls connect because your issues mirror ones they've struggled with. You have a lesson to learn and they have a reason to teach it.

On the darker side, some may resent your presence in their space and make that resentment known. You're in their home, on their property, using their things, or maybe even with their loved one. Just as the living must sometimes learn to move forward, those spirits who are still holding on too tightly to the past need to be told that better things lie ahead for them as well.

Finally, some souls attach themselves to you because they want to feed off your light. Although spirits are made of energy, they may choose a host body to help them amplify and emit their energy. Tapping into a host body's emotional energies, for instance, allows the ghost to make its presence, rage, anger, and fear known, and in some cases, even enables it to make physical objects move. When a ghost feeds off you in this way it can cause your light to dim and can also result in a wide variety of health issues, such as depression, lethargy, and weakness, among others. These are the entities you have to push back against and speak to firmly. Don't be afraid to stand your ground with them. Make sure they know that they're actually on *your* turf, that you have only enough energy for yourself, and that you're in control of what's happening through your own free will. Emphasize that *you* set the boundaries, *not* them. Be clear that they need to find their own light and not try to absorb that of other people. We'll talk more about specific ways to do that at the end of this chapter.

Mischievous souls are often children who are simply playing with you or hoping to find a surrogate family. Because their development is arrested, they have no idea how much fear they may be causing you. They just want to engage with you, to play games, to make a connection. It's especially important to help these souls turn toward the light so they can be reunited with their own family members waiting for them on the other side.

In other cases it can be the soul of what I call a *skutch*—someone who loves attention because they were never acknowledged enough while they were still alive. These are often sad souls, similar to the ones we all know and love. For example, the guy at a party who dances around with the lamp shade on his head the whole night. In this case, I would suggest treating this spirit the same way you would treat that annoying friend. Be loving but assertive. Let them know when enough is enough.

Malevolent souls are trapped spirits who can definitely cause harm. Some may want to resume life here so badly they attempt to inhabit you. They have some unfinished business and they need your body to complete it. Others express thoughts that permeate your thinking. They can sense a vice or habit you share—even if you've kicked it—and may try to entice you to resume it to justify their own past indulgences. They are hoping to get you to do something they'd like to do but can't. If you are aware of the presence of entities in your life pushing you to say and do things you don't mean to say or do, you must work with a true medium to help you cleanse your environment and send these souls on their way. Again, we'll spend time talking more about this shortly.

Of course, your own senses will indicate when energy is positive or negative. The air around you will change. The temperature will also shift. The butterflies in your stomach will run rampant when something is off. By contrast, you will feel an overwhelming sense of joy when something positive is in the air. In either instance you may not know why you're feeling the way you are. But trust that your intuition is as good a barometer as any. If you really listen to it, it will guide you.

Because I have met just about every kind of soul and have heard every kind of story, I always suggest you think about why this soul might be present. I also suggest you don't jump to judgment about a soul's intentions too quickly unless it is unequivocally threatening or menacing. Gathering the facts and unraveling the meaning of your interactions with these souls can sometimes help both of you make giant leaps forward. As I have discovered many times over, things are not always what they appear to be. Some souls who frighten you at first may actually be there for your own good.

ALL THAT IS WELL AND GOOD, BUT HOW CAN SOMEONE COMPLETELY AVOID THESE TRAPPED SPIRITS?

Sometimes we want to talk only to the spirits we want to talk to. It's like those calls from telemarketers in the middle of dinner. The only conversations you want to have at dinnertime are with the invited guests at your table. If that's the case with you, know that avoiding a trapped soul is not always in your control, but there are places you should stay away from or places where spiritually protecting yourself before entering is a good idea.

Before I discuss those places, let me just say that there are some trapped souls who don't want to have anything to do with you until you bother them. The ones attached to a specific place, for instance, may just want to remain there in peace. These souls tend to stay out of the way of everyday foot traffic. In the home, the most common places they hide are in attics, basements, empty garages, toolsheds, and rooms that are left unoccupied for months or even years at a time.

Now, for the places you'll want to enter with caution:

Cemeteries and burial grounds: These grounds can be a hotbed of activity. If a soul didn't go home to the light, it doesn't matter that his tombstone says he died a hundred years ago—he may still be out and about. Apparitions of people are often seen in and around these areas. Sometimes these departed souls know that their bodies are buried, yet they can't seem to understand why people aren't noticing their presence. Before you enter these places, wish these roaming spirits peace and a safe return to the light. Always know the customs of those who were laid to rest there and approach these grounds respectfully. God help the person who carouses and drinks in a cemetery, defiles the property, or even thinks about grave-robbing!

For the most part, however, my experience with transitioned souls (TSs) is different. The only time they hang around where their body has been laid to rest is when they see you standing near their gravesite with thoughts of them. Whether your heart is filled with grief or you are simply acknowledging a special day or memory, don't be surprised if you feel a slight touch on your shoulder or a light breeze around you on a very still day. They want you to feel their presence to ease your pain. In a nutshell, the majority of souls in a cemetery only get the call to appear when they hear the news that you'll be there.

Battlefields: Bear in mind that many people who died in battle did so fighting for a cause. They may still be in fighting mode, mistakenly viewing you as the enemy. If you appreciate their valor and ideals, you can mentally let them know this. If you don't, stay away or refrain from judgment while you're there. Know too that some people have been drafted into battles they had no desire to be in, so it is often best to remain a neutral observer at these historic sites.

Mortuaries or morgues: Just as in the case of cemeteries, every kind of spirit passes through these places: people who have been senselessly murdered, raped, or shot or have committed suicide— you name it. The variety of lingering souls can be too many to sort through. Here too you must enter with peace and love in your heart and wish that every soul finds its way home. This is a good thing to do in general when you find yourself in a place where you sense intense energy.

Hospitals: The same is true with hospitals, hospices, and long-term care facilities such as nursing homes. People exert so much will around surviving illness that it may take some souls time to realize that their body has given up the fight. There are always a few who remain behind because of this or because they are concerned about how their loved ones are coping. Emergency rooms are another place where trauma victims may stay for a while before going to the light. Confusion is one factor that may keep them there, but so too is anger at their assailant, or a determination to see the mystery behind their fatal injuries solved.

Prisons: Some who have died in prison remain behind because they may fear further judgment and repercussions for their crimes on the other side. Others may still be struggling with having been falsely accused. They may continue to look for a voice to defend or clear their name. Others may be holding on to the anger or hurt that caused them to commit their crime in the first place or they may be holding on to those same emotions due to the horrors they experienced during incarceration. Because prisons are occupied by souls who are restless in this life, they are places where I find some of the most unsettled souls after death.

Asylums: The souls trapped here have had untold anguish in their lives. The term *tortured souls* truly applies here. Many have endured such inhumane treatment at the hands of others that it is unthinkable. They have experienced everything from scientific experimentation, beatings, sexual assault, and starvation to complete and utter neglect. Those that stay behind have deeply complex issues to resolve. Some desperately want to expose the atrocities they suffered when they weren't mentally or physically able to defend themselves as a means of protecting or defending others still there. As some of you know, I visited Pennhurst Asylum, in Spring City, Pennsylvania, several times and one trapped soul attached to me. What haunts me to this day is not this soul but the things he revealed to me about what was done to him and others in his time there.

There are valid reasons for some people to visit prisons and asylums but I just have to say to the rest of you who think it's a great way to spend a night out with friends, these places are no laughing matter. There are some very famous, now-defunct prisons that offer overnight stays for the curious, and, even more frightening, asylums that are treated as Halloween attractions. I wouldn't be tempted to play in these places. They are not at all for fun and games and can give the phrase "trick or treat" a new meaning. If you don't know how to interact with these souls, stay away, or you just may get tricked.

HOW EXACTLY DO YOU HELP A TRAPPED SOUL FIND THE LIGHT?

What I love about this part of my work is there's really no great mystery about it. You don't have to be a medium or have any special skills when freeing the average trapped soul. Anyone can help them on their way. The simplest rule is tell them that it is okay to leave, that they will be safe, and that you are sending them into the light with love. Just as I am encouraging you to replace fear with love in your own life, you can encourage the trapped souls you encounter to do the same.

If you ultimately discover that this soul's reason for being around you is to help you in some way, be sure to thank them for their guidance. Acknowledging their good deeds will help raise their vibrations.

In the event the presence around you is a darker entity—one that may be more difficult to root out of your space—don't be afraid to be firm with it. Speak to it with the same commitment and authority you'd use when speaking to a stubborn child you're trying to get to listen to you—a child whose safety and well-being you are trying to preserve. Tell it in no uncertain terms that it is not welcome in your space and that it must leave. If it is persistent, you may want to use the protective power of certain crystals, which pack their own potent energies. I find that black obsidian stones work very well in these situations. Scatter them in the space where you are frequented by these entities. Light several white candles around them and repeat your demands for their removal several nights or days in a row. Be sure to leave a window or door partially open for them to leave through. Personally, I do not believe in kicking any soul (on this plane or the next) when it is down. For this reason, I highly recommend that as you are sending trapped spirits on their way, you remind them that they are naturally a part of the Light Source of God and no matter what circumstances brought them to this point, forgiveness and love are always available to those who are willing to forgive themselves first. Finding our way back to the light can be done quickly or it can become a long process. The choice is up to each soul as it makes its way on its own individual journey.

Now I know some of you are thinking, "This is getting a little weird. I don't want any part of kooky spiritual rituals." I get it, I really do. But believe me when I tell you that over the years I have adopted only the rituals that are direct and really helpful to me. I respect my peers who may have different methods but I'm all about keeping my practices real and to the point so anyone can do them. I offer a few more rituals here that really do work.

Ways to Protect Yourself from Darker Entities That Make You Feel Uneasy

In addition to practicing the Bubble Meditation shared with you in chapter 2, you can always ask your deceased loved ones, angels, and spirit guides (who are also known as protector guides) to shield you.

The Archangel Michael, long held to be God's champion against all negative forces, can provide protection as well. I'm sure you've seen pictures of this formidable angel carrying a powerful, mighty sword. There are many formal prayers you can say to enlist his help, but I prefer to talk to him the way I always talk to Jesus and Mary—as a close friend and confidant. Simply tell him what your concerns are and ask that any energies that are not of God's love and light be removed from you and your path, and this powerful angel will comply.

One of my early teachers introduced me to the power of sage, which has been used more commonly than you may realize. White sage, in particular, has helped the Celts, Druids, and Native Americans clear spaces of negative emotional energies for centuries. You can purchase a sage smudge stick from any crystal store. Freestanding sage is usually burned in an abalone shell or in a clay pot. When you light it, its smoke is released into the air. Walk around the rooms where the visitations have occurred and, with a feather (which is usually sold together with the shell), spread the smoke around. Again, you should bid the spirit you are sending off peace and love. A window should be open for its clear exit. Many churches use frankincense and myrrh for the same reason. Each is said to have its own properties that help lift the spirits, restore the soul, and relieve suffering.

Also, if you feel as if a darker entity has followed you home from any of the previously mentioned places you may have visited, there is a very effective *Shower Meditation* you can do. Yes, you read that right: trapped souls can and often do follow people home. They may not be so good at finding the light, but the only GPS they need on earth is you. You can get them from one place to the other very easily, just like the way the immigrant family from Ozone Park followed me to Commack. So as you lather up in the shower, visualize the bubbles capturing any negative energies that may have entered your space recently by piggybacking onto you. Now picture the warm water falling on your body as if it is a beautiful white light of love and divine protection. Imagine that this light is cleansing all of the dirty energy from your body, rinsing it right down the drain. It really is that easy. Voilà, squeaky-clean energy!

To continue to keep your space free of any returning negative energies, keep selenite, black tourmaline, or rose quartz crystals around your home. We will discuss these crystals, their powers, and their proper use and care, along with several other effective crystals in later chapters, but for now just know that keeping these particular gifts from nature can keep the energy in your home balanced and clean.

By the way, you don't have to wait to encounter an earthbound soul or negative energy to cleanse your environment and make it more comfortable for you. Many people moving into a new home use sage as described earlier so the energy in their home is all their own and not that of the people who may have lived there before them. I wonder how different things might have been had my family protected us all before moving into our new home.

Similarly, you may use lavender essential oil mixed with

water. Pour it in a spray bottle and spritz it around the room, especially in the corners. Parents may also spray lavender water in their newborn's nursery to clear the air before bringing their baby home.

GETTING CAUGHT UP IN THE WHIRLWIND

While crystals containing the powerful energies of the earth can often be used to help protect us against unwelcome spirits, sometimes it's the earth itself that attracts these spirits, which brings me back to the paranormal phenomenon I witnessed in my house in Commack. There are some places in nature that just seem to draw spirits to them in droves. Certain man-made structures and people can do the same thing. These powerful spiritual pulls create whirlpools called *vortexes*. For some reason the magnetic, gravitational, spiritual, or other force of these lands, structures, or people is so great that souls stuck between dimensions get attracted to and sucked into these energetic eddies. Sometimes these vortexes are actually *portals* to the other side. I suspect that my home in Commack, the land it was built on, or even my untrained psychic abilities served as a kind of vortex. There were just so many trapped souls there.

Vortexes are not as uncommon as you may think. But some exist on such a grand energetic scale that tourists travel to experience their energy. Having been to a few of these locations, I can tell you that you can be just as influenced by the positive energy that resides in some of them as you can be by the negative energy of others. Some of the most famous grand-scale vortexes abroad include the Egyptian pyramids and Stonehenge. In the United States there is the Oregon Vortex, the four vortexes in Sedona, Arizona, and the Superstition Mountains in Phoenix, Arizona, among many others. The energy of these sites can attract very high vibrations. Years ago, it was at a vortex in Sedona where I had one of my first intense spiritual experiences with one of the great ones, my childhood friend—the Blessed Mother Mary. She channeled through me leaving messages of hope for the world. Friends gathered around while tears of the Mother streamed down my cheeks, expressing her heartache for all the abuse our beautiful Mother Earth has suffered and endured at the hands of others. I haven't heard from her in this way since then, but she's always there when I need a friend or an ear. There is also the Mount Shasta vortex in Northern California, where Carnie Wilson and I met.

The recording studio where Carnie experienced a haunting was not only located in a building that had once been a mortuary, but was also in the highly charged town of Mount Shasta. Artists who worked in this studio often had extreme experiences—either enjoying complete creative inspiration or struggling with some of their worst demons. What is interesting about vortexes in general is that they can literally play with your perspective of reality—your physical as well as your emotional reality. For instance, in places like the Superstition Mountains the difference in gravity actually makes objects appear to be rolling uphill, and in the studio Carnie visited, the spirit she feared wanted to hurt her was actually a family member (albeit one with a stern presence while he was alive) who wanted to help her. The as-of-yet-unexplained power of these strange vortexes tells me that there is still a lot about energy that confounds us. As much as we know now, there are still countless mysteries we have yet to solve.

Chapter 4

Listen Up

Exercising Intuition and Building Faith

AFTER LEAVING COMMACK MY family moved to Valley Stream, Long Island, where the most miraculous thing happened to me. For the first time in as far back as I could remember, I no longer had random visions of ghosts. I couldn't believe it. I was able to get a good night's sleep and wake up refreshed in the morning *alone* in my room. There weren't countless people vying for my attention during the daytime anymore, or popping up in front of my face just as my head hit the pillow in the evening. I was finally living a normal life—if normal is even possible for a kid in her late teens.

In those days I loved to dance. I was a total disco queen. I would go to the clubs on weekends with my cousin Carmela and one of my closest girlfriends, Valerie. Probably the only thing I loved to do more than dance was laugh, and when I was out with those two I got to do a lot of both. One day Carmela (I call her Carm) told me about a guy she thought would be perfect for me. He and Carm attended the same trade school and she decided to play cupid. "I swear, Kim, you two are going to look gorgeous together," she said. "He's funny and nice and, oh yeah, he's kind of tall, and I know you like tall guys." I wasn't really interested at first, but my cousin's persistence was never ending, and besides, she always had such reliable instincts.

Carm was right, as usual. This guy and I hit it off and began dating almost immediately. He lived in Queens, just like my cousins, so when he wanted to see me he would take a cab out to Long Island. It would cost him forty dollars each way, which was a lot of money for someone his age. I just thought, "He must really like me," and truth be told, I *really, really* liked him too.

Most of the time we'd just hang out at my house and watch TV. I thought I had found the perfect match for myself. He was even born in Italy, just like my dad, so I figured that would allow for easier bonding and some leniency on my father's part. However, my father was still very strict about dating. He made it clear that if we went to the movies we had to be home at a certain time, no matter what. Neither of us seemed to mind, though. My mother would make us dinner and we'd eat together. She really liked him and to top it all off, we later learned, he was a phenomenal dancer. If I tell you he moved like Fred Astaire, I'm not exaggerating. Whenever we went to a family wedding he'd do the Lindy, the fox-trot, and even the waltz with my mom. I have no idea how he knew all the steps, but he did. The two of them were mesmerizing on the dance floor, and everyone would stop to watch them.

Everything was so nice for a while. But when this boyfriend finished school and started working evening hours at his job, the relationship began to change. I would still go to the clubs with Carm and Valerie. I had my dad's permission to do that because he knew the whole group of us, including my other cousins, were watching out for one another and that I was really just there to dance and be with my friends. If only this boyfriend could have been as relaxed about me going out with my peeps as my father was in that situation, everything would have been fine. But instead he called and asked a hundred questions: "Where are you?" "Who are you with?" "What are you doing?" Even when I told him I was with family and I wasn't doing anything wrong, he'd still say, "I don't want you out. I want you home. If you love me, you won't go to those places without me." The whole relationship started to become very conditional, very possessive, very out of control. Now I'm not talking one or two days—this became a way of life with this guy. And it was very unhealthy. Especially because I let it go on for way too long. There came a time when I didn't feel very safe with him while he was ranting and raving. There is an insecure side to almost everyone in their first relationship, and when you're that young your hormones only make things worse. But you still have to learn to control your jealous impulses, no matter what your age or experience.

Despite all the craziness, I was crushed when we finally broke up for the last and umpteenth time. It really doesn't matter who severs the ties—it always hurts. I remained depressed for many months, almost a year, afterward. But one of the biggest lessons this relationship taught me is that I definitely needed to guard against other people's energies overwhelming my own, especially since I am so empathic. When you find yourself either bending to another's will or rebelling against it strongly, it's a sure sign that your energies are at odds. *Setting firm boundaries for myself had to be a priority, whether I was dealing with the passions and differing viewpoints of a very possessive first boyfriend . . . or with those of an equally frustrated and confused trapped soul.* Energy is energy whether it belongs to the living or those in spirit. It's important to distance yourself from the energies that stifle your own.

As often happens when we have such a tumultuous experience, we can move in the exact opposite direction next time around. That was definitely true in my case. I was in my early twenties when Carm and I were out again one night at a different club and I started dancing with this guy who clearly didn't look like my type. My cousin saw this and instantly thought, "Uh-oh, I've got to get over there and rescue Kim." So she wriggled her way in, but much to her surprise, when she got to me I whispered in her ear, "I don't need any help. This guy is *hysterical.*" He was an accountant from Brooklyn—a CPA for one of the big eight firms. And if you want to talk numbers, on a scale of one to ten, his sense of humor was hands-down an eleven. We talked on the phone a few times, though, before we finally decided to go on a date.

I was feeling very nervous after the volatile relationship I previously had, so I invited my friend Valerie to come with us. At first, she was not having any of it. "What am I going to do while I'm at dinner with the two of you? Hold the candle?" she joked. I told this guy about asking Valerie to come with us, and while I could tell he was a little taken aback, he laughed at what she'd said. So what do you think he brought when he came to pick us up? In one hand he had a gift for me—a truly beautiful diamond tennis bracelet. It was a way more extravagant gift than I ever would have expected! In the other hand he had a present for Valerie. Yes, you guessed right: it was a candelabra! We all laughed. It totally broke the ice. That's how smooth this guy was—genuinely nice and very suave.

The whole time we dated he did things like that. He treated me like a princess. He always made the reservations for dinner or he'd surprise me by saying, "We're going out. Put on a nice black dress, and that's all I'm going to tell you." In time he bought me an engagement ring and a gorgeous two-bedroom town house for us to live in after we got married. It wasn't until after *he* broke off our engagement that I realized how wrong for each other we were. When he delivered the news, he said he didn't think I felt the same way about him that he felt about me. I was devastated but deep down I think I knew what he meant. I loved his spontaneity and his big heart, but something was missing. It just was. I would keep trying to convince myself that he was good for me, that we'd have a nice life together. But I wasn't being truthful with myself and I couldn't *not* be truthful forever. Especially because we were about to make a forever kind of commitment.

Although I hadn't been visited by spirits in a long time, I definitely felt connected to the other side after our breakup. I was very aware that a guardian angel had stepped in to help me avoid a very serious mistake. I kept feeling as if this angel had a really strong message for me in all of this. I think I was being told to listen more to my inner voice. My intuition signaled several times that marrying this person wasn't the right path to take, yet I ignored it until his intuition told him the same thing.

I've come to understand that we *all* have intuition. As I said before, Carm definitely has it in spades. (I even think that the intuition to get me and my first boyfriend together was on target, as there were things I needed to learn from that experience.) I have intuition too, and so do you. It's always there, along with the countless other thoughts that occupy our minds. Let me share a method that can help you recognize yours.

Listening to the Mother of All Psychic Senses: Intuition

With all the incoming messages your mind receives you almost have to have caller ID so you can screen for Intuition's messages, otherwise it may be too easy to miss them. I have found that a great way to get to know the sound of its ring is to set up a regular phone call with it. What I mean by that is set aside some time to quiet your mind. Before you do, pick a topic you may be wrestling with and let Intuition know that this is what you'd like to talk about when you meet. As you sit down to listen, treat the session like a private call. In the beginning it's not a good idea to talk to Intuition while making dinner or trying to put the kids to bed. As you get to know each other better you'll be able to converse with it whenever you need to. But for now stay behind closed doors where the only things you can hear are each other's voices. I feel compelled to tell you this because so many of us take important calls while multitasking these days, but this is not a time when you can get away with that. As you sit in silence, push away any unwanted, intrusive thoughts stemming from the ego mind and listen to whatever pops into your head on the topic you picked to discuss. Note: Intuition is more like knowing and *feeling* rather than *thinking rational thoughts*. Many times your fearful (or ego) mind can taint the true answer to your question. The ego mind says, "I know what's best for me," while your intuition comes from a higher wisdom that suggests, "I surrender to whatever outcome is best for all concerned." When you begin to trust the answer that is unexpected and makes the least sense to you, your intuition is most likely talking. You will be surprised at how clear the answers to your questions become over time. You may find yourself mulling over a problem without having directly asked Intuition to help, and out of nowhere you will hear an answer you didn't expect. When that happens you know you've learned to recognize Intuition's call—her ringtone, so to speak. Sometimes the process works in reverse. Intuition will call to ask us a question it believes we should think about, the way it kept asking me about whether or not I should marry my fiancé. I heard the questions but didn't give the answer enough serious thought. It was as if I put Intuition on hold. Had I recognized the voice I might have stopped to really think why it was asking the question.

This whole dialogue with Intuition works a lot like prayer, which brings me to the discussion of yet another relationship I worked on during my dating years.

REVISITING MY RELATIONSHIP WITH GOD

After my first horrible breakup, I began to attend church more frequently with my mother. She had a dear friend who was like an aunt to us. This woman's son had been involved in a devastating car accident. His recovery was long and extremely difficult. Though he overcame many odds, he was never really the same after that. To help her through those dark times, she became a born-again Christian. She gave her life over to Christ and received so much relief from her pain and worries that she wanted to share the blessings of her faith. She strongly believed that you have to get saved and give your heart to the Lord or you won't be able to enter the kingdom of heaven, so she encouraged my mother to go to this church with her. Although my mom had always attended Catholic mass, she found something different in these services she hadn't experienced before, and the change in her was instantly noticeable. She was always loving, but now she was easygoing too. There was just this peace about her. It seemed as if there was no problem or concern she couldn't conquer. She was always singing around the house. On Sundays she'd come home after church and everything was just blissful. The change was so positive that I went to this new church with her one day. In fact, the whole family started to go with her. And you know what? We really liked it. I thought, "Wow. I get such a nice feeling when I walk out of here." The services uplifted me and gave me hope. I loved it, loved it, loved it. We sang all these great songs and praised Jesus. The only thing that took some getting used to was raising my hands up to the heavens, because I had never done that in church before. But the people were all so loving and giving that I found myself drawn to the whole experience.

I soon started attending the youth group meetings every Friday night. It was a prayer group so I was very comfortable there. Jesus was always my confidant, my friend, my buddy. I knew the power of God from the time I was little because I'd seen it so much in my life, but these meetings were still eye-opening. I kept hearing everyone say that God has a plan for my life and nothing happens by chance. They'd tell one another, "Never underestimate what God can do. He can help heal your heart." Given that my heart had just been crushed, these were comforting words. Although this church didn't believe in the saints whose stories I loved so much, and they only talked about the Blessed Mother at Christmastime, I still thought it was fabulous. After giving my heart to the Lord and being baptized in the Holy Spirit I soon found that there was nothing you could throw at me that I couldn't handle. And that included a broken engagement a few years later!

There is one thing this church always said that has stayed with me to this day. Their teachings promise that if you give your heart to the Lord, he will never let you go. He'll let you stray for as long as you need to but you are always going to come back looking for him. This spoke directly to the huge struggle I harbored for many years regarding my gift of seeing spirits. I always knew the Catholic Church disapproved of talking to ghosts and I also knew born-again Christians disapproved of the practices of psychics and mediums. We were right alongside sorcerers, soothsayers, and fortune-tellers. I'm no Bible scholar, but I knew from the readings that were selected and from the sermons that were given that talking to the dead was strictly forbidden. It was the equivalent of talking to the devil. They would drill it into you that the devil always shows up as the light until whatever form he takes brings you down to his level of darkness. We were told repeatedly, "Don't be fooled by him. He can show up as your boss, your friend, or the most loving person you know." But what this line that stuck with me meant was that if seeing spirits was straying from God in some unwilling, unconscious way on my part, then being baptized in the Holy Spirit meant the Lord would always take me back.

I would talk with my mother about this concept much later as the abilities I was suppressing emerged more and more. Although she was very faithful, she was never fanatical about her beliefs. For example, the church preached that you shouldn't gamble or smoke, yet my mother did both because she suspected the Lord understood that certain enjoyments in life had their place.

When I finally became a medium and told her how much joy and relief I brought to the people I read for, she assured me that it's all in how I used my gifts. If people were crying tears of joy, finding peace in their hearts, and saying they were finally able to sleep knowing their loved ones were okay, as they were all telling me, then she thought the Lord was probably just fine with what I was doing.

I actually feel as if my gift was enhanced because my heart was opened. My spirituality and closeness with God made that gift *stronger* not weaker. But it took me a very long time to come to that conclusion. These early days in the church began my process of acceptance, but many more events had to unfold before I could truly embrace my gift.

FATHER FRANK DELIVERS THE GOOD NEWS

One of the events that helped me get over this hurdle once and for all wouldn't happen for another decade, but it's definitely worth mentioning here. A friend of mine, Pat Longo, went to a psychic fair where she heard about an ex-priest who was now a psychic. She got his card and convinced me we needed to go see him.

Although my mother had many psychics visit our house over the years, I think I had only one other reading before I met Father Frank. (Ironically, that psychic told me I would write a book one day!)

So Pat and I drove all the way out on Long Island to Suffolk County. When she called to make the appointment she was careful not to say anything about me. She didn't even mention my name. When Frank answered the door he was not at all what I expected. He had this big, black head of hair; a bushy, black mustache; and a full, robust body; and to top it off he had on this colorful *Hawaii Five-O*–style shirt. I'll never forget it. He had a total "Hakuna Matata" vibe going on. We agreed that he would read me first, so I followed him into the kitchen. On the table was a regular deck of playing cards. He told me to shuffle them. Then he said, "Let me explain my gift to you." I told him I was intrigued to hear about it because I understood he had been a priest before. He said, "Yes, I was, but God imparted the gift of knowledge to me." I probed further. "Are you a medium?" "No, I have the gift of *knowledge*, but if bringing through dead relatives provides you with knowledge then I can be a medium in that moment. *Knowledge*, however, is my gift. I just know things. They're told to me." I was totally cool with that and just curious to see what he knew about me. After I finished shuffling the deck of cards he began flipping them over one at a time. There was the six of diamonds, followed by the six of clubs. He paused for a minute and said, "Oh, well, now, look at this."

"What?"

"You're trying to deny the gift God has given you."

He got my attention, but I wasn't about to say or imply anything either way. I had my poker face on. I wasn't even making eye contact with him. I was looking at the cards like "Really? Where does it say that?"

He turned over a few more cards and said, "My dear, you came here with a great mission and a great purpose but you're having an internal struggle right now." He was right about the struggle. For all the comfort being baptized and knowing that God would take me back provided, over the years I had come to this point where doubt started creeping back in, but I didn't let Frank know this. He kept talking vaguely about this gift God had given me. I just couldn't take it anymore so I finally said, "Listen, I don't mean to be rude. I consider myself as having a lot of gifts. I'm creative; I can sew, which my grandmother taught me to do; I keep a nice, clean house; and I have a keen eye for decorating. I don't really know what this gift is that God gave me. Do you think you could be a little more specific?"

He gave a little chuckle. He knew I knew exactly what he was talking about but that I wanted more details. So he turned over a few more cards. "It's very clear to me what your gift is. You have the gift of talking with dead people."

I had to know where in those cards it said that so I pressed him about it. "Where? Where does it say that?"

"I have the gift of knowledge and I see that you are able to raise your vibration—people's dead relatives are able to lower their vibration and you're meeting them in the middle to bring those messages back from the dead."

I was in complete awe. I nearly fell off my chair. Just by looking at me, you would never know I talked to dead people, or as I like to say— they talked to me. For all he knew, I could have worked in a hair salon or behind a makeup counter in Bloomingdale's. Where in God's name did he make this connection? "Frank, how do you know that?" I said. He laughed again and asked, "Do you talk to the dead?"

"Yes. Yes, I do. You can put the cards away because I don't need more of a reading. I have a million questions for you."

He smiled broadly. "Shoot. I'm all ears."

I got right to the point. "How does my gift fit into the Bible?"

He started quoting me all this Scripture. It was so eloquent and liberating it made my hair stand on end. The experience was so profound; I'll never forget it. He quoted passages in proof of the afterlife and in proof of the invitation to do light work, such as in John 3:16,

"For God so loved the world that he gave his only Son, so that everyone who believes in him may not perish but may have eternal life," and John 14:12, "Very truly, I tell you, the one who believes in me will also do the works that I do and, in fact, will do greater works than these, because I am going to the Father."

Then he asked, "Do people walk away from your readings with fear? Do they feel horrified? Do they leave with more questions than they came in with? Or do they walk away with a lighter heart? With peace in their heart? With knowledge that they didn't have before—knowledge that gives them the tools to move forward?" I couldn't believe it. That was what I was hearing from people almost verbatim.

"If so, that's all you need to know, Kim. You're doing God's work. When you impart peace in people's hearts and you leave them with joy and love, that's God. That's nobody but God. The devil will never give you peace. The devil will never impart love and the devil will never impart wisdom that can heal a heart."

You want to talk about an aha moment. Fifty million lightbulbs went off in my head. The most simplistic answer changed my life. That *was* all I needed to know. And from that conversation I never turned back. I went full steam ahead. I also made it a point to always, always, always begin my readings by asking God to help me serve the highest good of all those involved. This assures that I am only delivering messages of peace, love, and wisdom according to the Divine Source.

There is one more thing, however, that I remember from that reading. When we were talking about channeling, Frank quipped, "How do you think most of the Bible was written, Kim?" It kind of leaves you wondering.

ONE TABOO THE CHURCH AND I AGREE ON

Because talking to Spirit is not to be taken lightly or considered a game, there is one practice most mediums and clergy agree is dangerous to pursue. Playing with Ouija boards and/or conducting séances can have serious consequences. These are forms of interactions with the dead that are wild cards. When you invite unknown souls into your life you never know what you will get. The randomness of these practices can unleash spirits too dark and troubled to contend with—trapped souls with the lowest vibrations, including spirits that once did unspeakable things ranging from rape and torture to murder. Most participants have no clue what to do once a spirit presents itself. In their naïveté they are opening up a channel for more than one such troubled soul to get through at the same time. And they are doing so without any prior knowledge of how to close the door on that portal.

One of the worst offenses is when participants ask the souls for some physical proof of their presence. This not only opens the door wider, but invites spirits to run amok. It surrenders your space and physical property to them. During her episode of *The Haunting Of* . . . , Coco Austin talked about how she and her sister did this very same thing. It was no wonder the chandelier in their kitchen shook—it clearly took the power of more than one spirit to move an object of that weight and size. Those spirits remained in that house—I could feel their energy all around me as we revisited the place many years later.

I have said it before: I do not travel in the neighborhood of the lower astral plane, because I am not comfortable engaging with souls at those vibrations. But in order to know what neighborhoods to avoid, you need to have studied the map. You have to know the lay of the land and what wrong turns may lie ahead. I'm certain this is what the Bible is cautioning against, and in that case I wholeheartedly agree.

Chapter 5

Soul Contracts

How We're Bound to Fulfill Our Life's Goals

I'D BE LESS THAN honest if I said that the sudden appearance of ghosts when I was younger didn't make me want to know more about the afterlife. That the droves of spirits that showed up in my Commack house didn't make me insanely curious, or that the silence all throughout my dating years didn't make me wonder about the purpose of these ghosts' presence *and* absence.

You *now* know the reasons I didn't pursue them the way they pursued me: it wasn't so much that I was afraid of them as it was that I was afraid God would disapprove. But if you don't believe yet that God works in mysterious ways, check back with me by the end of these next few chapters.

DESTINY CALLS

I was home nursing that last blow to my heart—you know, the one where I was planning a wedding one day and the next day I wasn't. Even though my girlfriends kept asking me to go out with them I resisted. I'm pretty sure they thought I was depressed, but I actually stayed home because I was considering my next step in life. I was wondering if I should just date more—you know, not rush into another serious relationship so soon. Maybe all I needed was to give myself some time and space to see what else the world had to offer.

On this one night I gave in to the pressure to go out because my friend kept saying it would be good for me, but I suspected she really needed to get out herself. So I said, "All right. You know what, let's go." But this time we didn't head to the place we usually went to. We ended up at a much quieter local club. First we sat at the bar; then we danced a bit. I stopped in the ladies' room for a minute and then returned to the dance floor again. In that time I noticed a pattern. So I asked my friend, "See that guy with that girl?" She said, "Yeah."

"Well, tell me if I'm crazy but wherever I go I see him following me." She said, "Really? That's weird. He's with a girl."

"I know. It's bizarre, but he's really freakin' cute. Isn't he?"

She agreed, so we set up a little test to see if I was right. Sure enough, whenever we moved, he moved too, but opposite me to get a clearer view. So now my friend and I are sitting and talking, and although I'm generally not much of a drinker, I was on my second glass of wine. As the time passed, I saw that this guy was still staring at me. I don't know what possessed me. (Well, in retrospect I do.) But I thought, "I'm going do something totally out of character." So I wrote my phone number on a matchbook, and I told the bartender, "You see that guy across the way? Don't look now. Casually turn around. He's sitting with a girl over there. When she gets up to go to the bathroom, give him this number." Of course he was surprised—and not just because I was being forward. He said, "You know he's with her, right?"

I wasn't deterred. "I'm well aware of that, but she's obviously going to go to the bathroom at some point and when she does it would be great if you would just give this to him." No sooner had I said those words than she got up and went to the little girls' room. The bartender handed him the number, and all of a sudden I was dying. I had never done anything like this before in my life. It was completely unlike me. I got so shy I put my head down. My girlfriend kept saying, "Kim, Kim, lift your face. He's trying to make eye contact with you. If you don't, he's going to think the number is mine." With that thought I popped my head back up, and it was obvious he knew whose number it was. He mouthed the words, "I'll call you." I nodded, gave him a wink, and was out of there. That was it. Done.

The next night rolled along. I wasn't even thinking about what I'd done. I was in my room with the phone attached to my ear, as always, talking to one of my girlfriends when he called. We talked and he told me that the girl he was with the night before was not his girlfriend. He said he was doing a favor for her as a friend. She was depressed and he decided to take her out. Convinced that this was the oldest line in the book, I said, "Give me a break." But he continued. Now he thought that maybe she liked him and he wondered how he should let her down. I couldn't believe it. This guy wanted relationship advice from the woman he was staring at all night!

We laughed about that and he said, "Yeah, I'll figure it out." Then the conversation turned to a thousand other topics. I told him about my family, and he told me about his. There were so many parallels and yet we were very different. His home life was complicated, to say the least, but he seemed so normal. I found his story intriguing and I loved that he was so confident.

As we dated, I began to discover more qualities in him that fit my needs perfectly. So much for playing the field! You know the old expression: people make plans while God laughs. Well, God must have been having a very good chuckle because I began to really like this guy, and it was clear he liked me too. He had a heart of gold and yet he could not be pushed or manipulated by anyone to do anything he did not want to do. Although he was a teddy bear, he was not afraid of confrontation. And because he was sure of himself, he was okay with me being sure of myself as well. He never once tried to change or control me. This was definitely a new experience. He let me be me, and it made me feel so special that he was digging who I truly was.

Everything was going along so well when one day not even six months into our dating, he announced he was getting another tattoo. He had a couple already but this time he was having my name put on his arm. I begged him not to: "Please, *please* do not do this." I worried it would make me feel obligated and trapped. He simply said, "I'm doing it whether you want me to or not. It's my body." His conviction just blew my mind. He went on to explain, "I think we're dating; I think we're at a good place. It doesn't mean anything more than I feel for you to the point where I want to do this." When I asked, "What if it doesn't last?" he said the most amazing thing: "Well, then I'll need to deal with it, won't I?" That's how adamant he was. "If you want to come with me, come with me, but with or without your permission, Kim, I'm doing it. Whether we wind up together or not, you mean that much to me that I want your name on my arm no matter what happens."

I knew right then and there we were always going to be up-front with each other. We were going to be that honest because we were both the kind of people who could take it. *I had found my life partner.*

In time we married and raised three awesome sons, Nicholas, Joseph, and Anthony Jr. And yes, Anthony got his tattoo that day.

LEARNING FROM OUR LOVED ONES

The great thing about having a life partner is that he or she helps you constantly discover new things about yourself. My years between getting married and becoming a medium were filled with lots of self-discovery. In addition to starting a family and actively studying psychic phenomena, I had many other life-altering experiences, which I will fill you in on as we go along. But for now I want to jump ahead several years to that time when Anthony and I were exploring past lives together, as I talked about in chapter 1, because it really does explain so much about relationships—mine with Anthony as well as yours with the significant people in your life.

By the time I conducted my first regression, I had already developed a number of my psychic skills but was still very reluctant to use them.

Looking into past lives just seemed safer to me than talking to spirits. Somehow it felt like I was investigating within acceptable boundaries. Since I knew the Church believed in life everlasting I thought it would be okay with God to explore the soul history of a *living* person, especially a person I knew and loved so much. It was different than mediumship. Or so I thought . . .

THE FIRST OF THREE BOLD MESSAGES

Believe me, no one was more surprised than I was when after hearing about Anthony's lives as a sea captain, a math teacher, and so forth, he stopped talking as himself and began channeling spirits from the other side to talk to me *through* him!

The first time it happened, I got to speak to my grandmother. It was almost like a warm-up conversation—a practice session. We were doing the exact same thing we always did, when all of a sudden Anthony said, "Susie's here." At first, I wasn't making the connection. So naturally I asked, "Who's Susie?"

When he said, "Nana," I thought, "There's no way."

I didn't know where talking to her might lead, but I went along with it just the same.

"Hi, Nana."

"Hi, Kim."

(By the way, whenever Anthony is under, his voice is always monotone. It was interesting to note that there was no inflection even when he spoke as someone else.)

"How are you?" I asked.

"I'm really good."

"What are you doing over there? Who are you with?"

"Sam. I'm with Sam."

It was odd that she didn't just say, "Your grandfather." He died the year before I was born, so I never met him, but I definitely would have referred to him that way. As I was thinking this I heard her say, "Sam, go wash your hands before dinner. Get the ink out from under your fingernails."

Now I knew my grandfather was a printer, but I didn't think that was a detail I ever told my husband. Hearing this made me fairly certain Anthony's subconscious mind wasn't the one providing this information.

"What does that mean, Nana? Why did you say that?"

"He has to wash his hands. They're dirty from ink."

It wasn't a big, momentous conversation we were having. We spoke a little bit about my aunt who is my mother's younger sister, and who is my godmother as well. But somehow I suspected the comment about my grandfather and the ink was a clue of some kind.

It was midnight and I knew my mother would still be awake, so I called her.

"Hi, Mom. Don't get nervous. Everything is okay. Remember that thing I do with Anthony sometimes? When I put him under hypnosis? Well, Nana came through. She said something to Grandpa before they sat down for dinner. I don't want to tell you what it is because I want to see if I'm getting it right."

"Oh my God. Grandma used to bug my father to no end about his fingernails. He was not allowed to sit down to the dinner table until he washed the ink out from under them."

I said, "Mom, you're not going to believe what's going on here. Nana just told me that."

That's when my mother asked, "Kim, do you really think you should be doing this to your poor husband? Isn't he exhausted in the morning?" I knew she was right, so I quickly ended my conversation with her and resumed talking to Nana.

"Listen very carefully, Nana. I'm pretty sure you're talking to me through my husband, Anthony. Please tell me how I can talk to you directly. I don't want to use Anthony to have conversations with you. I want to talk to you without his help."

Her answer was simple and I instantly understood it on the most basic level, but I wasn't to understand it fully until years later when I explored different energies and started working with chakras. She said, "Open your heart." And that is how the lessons from Spirit started.

MESSAGE 2: MORE INSIGHT FROM LOVED ONES

Since Anthony was my partner on this unusual journey of discovery, the spirit world had a validation for him too.

One night Anthony's grandfather, Tony, came through and began talking to me directly. He told me that the next morning I was to ask Anthony what he used to affectionately call him when he was a child. The nickname he supplied was one Anthony had never shared with me. He called Anthony Antonio Passaquai. Passaquai is a slang word in Italian loosely translated as "here comes trouble." He also relayed details of a game he and Anthony played together on their weekly visits to the candy store. Again, because I wanted to be sure all of this was not coming from Anthony's subconscious, I asked his grandfather to help prove that this was not just one of Anthony's memories resurfacing. What he said to me in response was a bit mysterious.

"Ask him about the radio—about the song on the car radio. And just tell Anthony that it was me."

Anthony's reaction was typical: "What? You did it again?" By now, Anthony had given me blanket approval to talk to Spirit through him whenever I wanted, but he never had any recall of our sessions.

"Yes, but listen. I'm happy I did. Guess who came through?"

"Who?"

"Your grandpa. And he told me the nickname he used to call you when you were little—Passaquai. I know all about the bubble gum game too." Now this freaked Anthony out.

"He told you that?"

"Yes, and he told me to ask you about what happened with the car radio and the song. He said that was him."

At this point you have to know that I had never seen my husband cry in all the years we'd been married. He gulped, and as he did I caught a glimpse of this little tear streaming down his cheek. He told me he heard this song on the radio a few days earlier while he was driving to work. It was a song that his grandpa used to sing. Although he changed the station several times, he kept getting that song. It immediately brought back a flood of memories. He thought maybe the car radio had a short. Of course, if that had happened to me it would have instantly dawned on me that a loved one was sending me a message. It would have been a no-brainer, but this is my husband we're talking about. And it was also well before I had fully developed my psychic gift and our world became even more consumed by spirits. He was busy thinking about how he had to get to work and support his young family. He was not thinking, "This is a sign from Grandpa." He was thinking, "This is a sign the car needs a tune-up." So this realization stopped him cold in his tracks. It really did.

His reaction was evidence enough for me that this message didn't come from Anthony. I was talking to a complete and separate intelligent entity who knew what I was saying and who was answering me *through* Anthony. And now Anthony knew it too. But to be sure he got the message, his grandfather came through to me again the very next night. He said, "Kim, please be sure to tell Anthony to check my phone number." Later that night I dialed the number he gave me and it rang and rang. Naturally, there was no answer. So I told Anthony. "I don't know why, but your grandfather wants you to call his number," and I handed him the one I had written on a slip of paper by my bedside. He asked incredulously, "What's this? How do you know this number?"

"He gave it to me."

"That's weird. I had it disconnected after my grandmother died, but I was on a job in the old neighborhood last week, and something came over me. I don't know why, but I called to see if it was still working. I got that recording. You know, the one that says, 'The number you're trying to reach has been disconnected.' And now you're telling me this."

"Well, I tried the number last night and it was an active line. There was no such recording," I said.

Now there was no doubt in my mind: Grandpa Tony saw Anthony reach out to him and he found a way to say, "Here's a phone number Kim could never possibly know—a number I saw you check just this week. This is proof I see you and am still here with you." It was code for *Whenever you need me you just have to call.* I didn't know Spirit could manipulate things like that. And while it was really spooking me out, I was loving every minute of it. These conversations with the other side were making the intangible very tangible. I knew I was in touch with another world. And this was just one more piece of evidence. Since both of these souls came to me and both were close relatives we really loved, I thought talking with them wouldn't jeopardize my standing with God.

MESSAGE 3: THE BOMB-DIGGITY-DOG OF ALL CHANNELING EXPERIENCES

But after Anthony brought through our respective grandparents, other spirits neither of us knew began filtering through. "Hi, my name is Joe." "My name is Kenny." "I fell to my death." "I took my own life."

I started to get a little nervous. I realized that our explorations were reaching a far deeper dimension. What dimension that was, I wasn't sure. To help Anthony get to this dimension more comfortably, I stopped using the past-life script we had used before and I simply put his conscious mind to sleep so he could become a channel for whoever wanted to filter through. I made sure to first guide him through the protection process, surrounding him with white light, before I began clearing the path for others from the spirit world to speak. And speak they did!

Before I tell you about one particular encounter, I must say that I respect all religions and I am genuinely not trying to push one view over another. Although I have spoken a lot about my Catholic background, and about having been raised in the Christ consciousness, I am of the opinion—given the kind of work I do—that all religions can lead to the same place. I believe there is one Divine Source, the Creator of all, which I will call God. Who we happen to invite into our heart—our spiritual home—to deliver God's message is just a matter of comfort. It comes down to which of these teachers' words gives you peace. We are each on a journey to find our truth, and along the way we'll receive many messages from many messengers. Those messages that are passed down the line from the Divine Source help further our journey. And I believe the messages I'm about to share ultimately came from a source of higher wisdom with divine knowledge, because they really have furthered my journey.

Very late one night, during a session, an unfamiliar voice announced herself using Anthony's vocal chords.

"Kali's here."

"I'm sorry, who's Kali?"

"I've been watching Anthony since he was a little boy. I am his protector."

"*Who* are you?"

"I am his spirit guide. I watch over him."

Now this was news to me. I was studying with an incredibly knowledgeable teacher at the time and while I had heard about such guides, I didn't know I could actually meet one. Can you imagine what was going through my head? I truly love my husband, but knowing him as I did, I was sure he'd never even heard of the term *spirit guide*. He wasn't the one reading all of the spiritual books. *I* was. His heart was into helping me, but his head wasn't into hearing all about it. He was working too hard to give his family everything we needed—the poor guy was holding down two or three jobs just to make sure we didn't go without. Although he supported my spiritual quest, I was positive he had no knowledge of such topics or of the terminology he was using while speaking in this trance. If I was talking to a spirit guide through him I had to find out more.

"Do I have a spirit guide too?"

"Yes, everyone does. Yours is Malick."

I kid you not—I asked her to spell his name as well as hers. I was not about to leave one bit of vital information on the table. In retrospect, I realized that it is extremely rare to be able to channel a spirit guide in this way. Think about what an amazing discovery this was. I felt like a kid on Christmas morning with a new toy. My very own Magic 8 Ball—or a genie in a bottle that could finally explain all the mysteries of the universe to me. It was like winning the lottery. For someone as inquisitive as I am, it was a total score. I had to engage. I also had to hope that I wasn't crossing a religious line I couldn't cross back over again. To be sure, I decided to put this spirit through its paces. I really grilled her. Initially I did it to see if she truly was who she said she was—that she was *not* the devil in disguise—and then I did it to learn everything I could from her.

By the way, I would later feel much more comfortable hopping over this "thin line" I was so concerned about, because what I was really engaged in was a scientific pursuit. I was trying to understand more about the nature of indestructible energy, which had nothing to do with faith or religion at all!

I must have asked Kali a hundred questions that night and on many other nights to follow. After several appearances and even more tests of her authenticity, I finally decided that this chick was for real. She had patiently answered every query and named me Curious Kim in the process. I'm not going to lie—at first I felt a weird sense of competition with this female who knew my husband so intimately, even before I did. Whenever I asked her questions regarding my life, her answer was always the same: "I'm not your guide, Kim. I am Anthony's." It always made me feel a little left out. I wanted to know where my guide was and how come he didn't speak to me through Anthony too. Her answer shocked me. She said, "He's helping others at this time."

That really set me off: "Helping others? What does that mean? Am I traveling solo? What the heck? Anthony has a twenty-four-hour security guard and I'm an open target?" Kali often got right to the point with me: "No, Kim. When Malick is busy, he always sends you other helpers." I thought, "Okay, I can accept that." But whatever was the case for me, I noticed that no matter what happened to Anthony, Kali always took charge. She never once left his side. I'm sure it's the same to this day, and for this I am truly grateful. As I probed further for proof of who Kali is, her answers offered snapshots of Anthony's life only a coveted few knew about.

Shortly after Anthony and I were married, one of Anthony's sisters, who already knew that she and her younger sister were adopted, found papers in their parents' closet that revealed all of the children in his family had been adopted, including him! He had been lied to all this time. It was hard for me to watch someone I love endure this kind of trauma—it caused such heartache. But thankfully Anthony was able to rise above it. Together we went on a mission to find his birth mother and we discovered the circumstances of his early life. Kali solved a few remaining mysteries for us on this subject and it soon became clear how Anthony was able to become the extraordinary person he is today against such stacked odds. Kali had, in fact, been watching over him all along!

What she had to say over the course of our sessions together is relevant to us all, not just to Anthony, which is why I'm including so much of what we learned in this and in subsequent chapters.

Life According to Kali

First Kali confirmed that each of us has lived many, many lives, some more adventurous than others. We were men in some lives, we were women in others, we've assumed several different nationalities and races, and we've practiced many different religions. We have worked in various professions and trades as well. When I later became a full-fledged medium I learned that records documenting all the lives we've lived actually exist and are accessible in the cosmic consciousness. These records are called the Akashic records and some mediums, such as me, have the ability to read them.

MORE ABOUT THE AKASHIC RECORDS

When they are accessed individually, the Akashic records offer us the most complete view possible of our past and present lives, as well as a view of our potential futures. Far more than a memoir, each record is an inexhaustible account of everything—and I mean *everything*—we have ever thought, said, done, or had done to us in this dimension or any other.

But these records are not just about us. Collectively they contain the same breadth of information for *every* soul who has ever lived. They are so all-encompassing that instead of being recorded on reams of paper they are recorded on Akasha, which in various ancient languages can be interpreted to mean anything from "infinite space" to the "primary substance" to "the essence of all things," and which today we understand to mean the purest energy. These are our permanent records in every sense of the word. They are intended to last for all eternity.

Some people refer to them as a record of all human existence. In both the Old and New Testaments, the Bible refers to them as the Book of Life. So yes, we've known about these records as far back as we can remember. Cultures including the Arabs, the Hebrews, the Greeks, the Chinese, the Mayans, and many, many others have written about it. You may have even heard it referred to as the Eye of God, the Conscious Mind, the Collective Unconscious, or even God's Remembrances. I like the latter term because, like the scrapbooks parents lovingly keep for their children, it is as if the Creator of all life is letting us know that nothing we do ever goes unseen. We are not invisible. Quite the opposite, we are always held in the Creator's view. That there is a place in the records for future possibilities means that we have a role in contributing to the scrapbook too.

In more modern times—during the early 1900s—the famed clairvoyant and Christian mystic Edgar Cayce not only accessed these records during his readings, but also shared insight into how he gained entry and what they contain, teaching a whole new generation of mediums how it is done. Although he induced a sleeplike trance, different clairvoyants have developed other methods, including a wide variety of meditations, prayers, and visualization techniques.

Although each of us has the potential to develop the skills

necessary over time to read our own records, many people turn to practiced mediums for help retrieving their files. Bear in mind, however, that mediums can get into your file only with your permission. None of us has unrestricted access to these records.

When I view people's files I can clearly see the calling they agreed to fulfill. For instance, if a young woman agreed to become a nurse in this lifetime, I will see that path for her. If she is off her intended path, I will not tell her what to do, but I will remind her of what she consented to. This news is never completely foreign to those I read for, because each person's soul already knows why they are here. They sometimes just need to pull this soul memory up from the subconscious to the conscious mind. Similarly, I can look at their relationships with their spouse, friends, coworkers, or boss, particularly if one of these relationships is not serving them well, and I can share with them the reasons this may be happening. I will see if the troublesome relationship is with someone they knew in a prior lifetime. If so, I will tell them if their karmic debt with this person is *not* yet finished, or if in fact it is complete, in which case they are free to move forward.

As you can see, the Akashic records are not just a tool for mediums. They are proof of one more way in which our mission here is supported by the divine.

Kali also explained that we come to each life with a purpose. We have a formal agreement—a contract—with the Divine Source to work on some aspects of ourselves that we didn't get right in a prior lifetime. According to the rules of the soul, one of the reasons we come here is to learn a particular set of karmic lessons unique to our past-life experiences. These are lessons intended to help us get closer to Enlightenment. *Enlightenment*, of course, means that we have finally merged with God. That we experience God—the source of everything that is *unconditional love*—within us and around us, not just with our five senses (mind and intellect), but with our heart and soul.

Kali also told me that each life is populated with some of the same people we've interacted with in a previous life. In order to achieve our goal of Enlightenment, we come here again to complete the give-and-take account we have with various others. These people who come here with us are collectively called our soul group. Kali very clearly stated that each member of our soul group chooses in advance to live among us to help us learn our stated lessons, or so we might help them learn theirs.

This certainly explains Anthony and my son Joseph's interesting relationship, which I mentioned in chapter 1. And it also explains Anthony's and my relationship. What I didn't tell you earlier is that during one of Anthony's more fun and revealing regressions, he revisited his former life with me. I was apparently his landlord at one time, and that's not all . . . We were lovers in that past life too. Clearly we were meant to live under one roof in this incarnation. As already seen and as you will continue to see in the chapters ahead, Anthony fulfills his role in this lifetime as the primary member of my soul group every day by his clear agreement to help me be all that I can be. I could not do what I do without his continuing love, patience, and support. My husband has not only been a committed family man who's obviously enabled me to fulfill my life goal of being a wife and mother, but also quietly and consistently helped me fulfill my goal of connecting people with their loved ones in the spirit world. Besides being a rare somnambulist and a willing party to past-life regression sessions, Anthony was the one for nearly twenty years who most often answered the phone when people called to schedule an appointment for a reading. It was his friendly manner that kept many of them calm and hopeful when they learned how long the waiting list was. It was his planning and juggling that got the people with the most urgent needs seen—parents who'd lost a child were always treated with extra care. His compassionate work as a volunteer firefighter and tireless labor as a cement mason with New York City's Department of Homeless Services also hints at our shared soul purpose of enlightening, uplifting, and helping to heal others.

In addition to telling me that the purpose of each life is to improve upon the soul so we might someday reach Enlightenment, Kali also explained to me that the Divine Source makes every resource available to us to help us achieve that purpose. Each of us, as mentioned earlier, has our own special spirit guide in the way Anthony has Kali. In addition to our soul group, we have a throng of angels, helper or teaching guides, master guides, and ascended masters available to help us too.

I've included a detailed description of their roles here just as they have been told to me.

YOUR OWN PERSONAL TEAM OF LIFE COACHES

Spirit guides: Again, one special spirit guide is assigned to each of us at birth and remains with us for life. Other spirit guides, known as helper guides, join at different points to supplement our main spirit guide's efforts. To understand this better, think about how you are taught in school: a kindergarten teacher doesn't typically instruct college-level courses for obvious reasons. As you grow you will need more advanced help from a specialist or someone with greater knowledge of a specific subject. Maybe your interest in golf has recently intensified. Your swing improved enough to make you think this might be more than a hobby. A deceased fan of the sport (someone who played every free moment they could), a longtime caddy, or perhaps a onetime PGA tournament player may end up being your helper or teaching guide from the other side. That's how this works. All spirit guides and their helpers have lived a prior life as a human. It's important that they have this earthly experience so they can help you navigate your emotions as they also help you accomplish your goals. While it is possible for them to be a family member who has passed on, more often than not they are an unrelated spirit who shares the same interests and talents, and has had similar opportunities or challenges as you have. This enables them to offer you tried-and-true advice.

Even though your spirit guide didn't necessarily live with you in a prior life, aligning with the right guide happens organically. It's a lot like entering a bookstore—you may not know the author you are looking for, but as you gravitate toward the subject that interests you, you just naturally find a title to fulfill that interest.

Angels: These very special beings live in heaven for real. Most of the angels who watch over us are called guardian angels, and they are supervised by angels even higher up in the hierarchy called Archangels. Are they floating on a cloud and playing a harp? No. But I will tell you they absolutely, absolutely, absolutely have beautiful angel wings. Not only did Kali tell me this, but throughout my work and study of people who have had near-death experiences, I have found that many survivors report the exact same thing: angels come adorned with magnificent wings.

It is true that angels also appear to us as humans to help us in distress. We've all heard stories about strangers coming out of nowhere to pull a driver from a burning car or to rescue a child from clear and present danger before disappearing almost as mysteriously as they arrived. But despite taking human form on occasion, angels have never actually been human. They are a species made by God specifically for heaven to help those in need throughout many different universes. These celestial spiritual beings are superior to humans in power and intelligence as they are made up of the pure light vibrating at a higher frequency of the God force.

One of the most amazing things about angels is there is at least one for just about every situation, big or small. There are angels who are charged with working for world peace, and there are others whose primary purpose is to help you find a parking spot. If you want joy in your life, simply ask the angels of joy to bring you some. Truly, there are angels to help you with *all* your needs—*but they cannot help you unless you ask*. They are not permitted to interfere with your free will. This a golden rule for all the life coaches. However, because we are constantly interacting with the free will of others, not just exercising our own free will, there may come a time when someone else's free will can potentially alter your life's purpose. It is then that exceptions to this rule can be made and angels are able to intervene on your behalf. Other exceptions can be made too, as I mentioned before. For instance, if someone is involved in a life-threatening situation where they could die before it's their time, our angels are granted special permission to come to our rescue. We have all heard remarkable stories of people's survival because of some weird delay in traffic or because a phone call kept them from being in a certain place at a certain time. That is surely your angel at work.

Master guides: These old souls have progressed far. These are the people who have done the spiritual due diligence required for a soul's growth. During their prior incarnations as humans their understanding of our existence has deepened to the point where their knowledge is actual wisdom. They exist to inspire and serve all of humanity, not just to help individuals. Mother Teresa, Gandhi, and Martin Luther King Jr. are all wonderful examples of these very advanced teaching spirits.

Ascended masters: Jesus and Buddha, among others, are examples of ascended masters. Not only do these souls *teach* the concept of love but they also *are* love. These enlightened beings are the highest teaching souls of all—the kind who help us become more greatly attuned to the infinite, who bring us closer to faith and an understanding of the source of all, the divine.

I'm a psychic so I can see that perplexed look on some of your faces. This is the part where you're thinking this is all too good to be true. *A source of love doesn't want me to feel alone or segregated from others? A powerful being is offering me help at every pass—and all I have to do is ask for it? Spirits really do have the big picture in view and they want to share it with me? The people in my life now are all really meant to be here to help me learn a vital lesson? How can Kim be so sure?*

I get it. Two decades ago I asked the same questions. But just look at the events of my life during my dating years. I always wondered why the ghosts left me alone during that period. It wasn't just a coincidence. It never is, and if you are like me, you believe there is no such thing as coincidence.

What I realize now is that in addition to the intuition I was ignoring and the guardian angel I became aware of after the fact, I had spirit guides looking out for me. Because these spirit guides were once human too, they understood that the late teens and early twenties are our formative years—that crazy period when we start sorting out what we're going to do in life and who we're going to do it with. They are the years when we really don't listen much to anyone else, because we have to figure out this important piece of the puzzle for ourselves. Remember the rule about free will Kali mentioned: No one can interfere with it. *Ever.* Although my guides knew exactly what my life missions were— the ones I signed on for before coming to earth—I had to somehow reconnect with those goals myself.

In my heart of hearts I know one of my missions in this life was to become a good wife and mother. Any distraction during my time

of discovering who was and wasn't the right person to help me fulfill that mission could have led me down the wrong path, especially
if my guides couldn't intervene. That's why I think they temporar-
ily banished the ghosts. They didn't want my attentions diverted in
any way that might lead me down a different road. I also believe
they had a strong hand in leading me to a place I rarely went to in
order to meet Anthony. They were there working behind the scenes
to guide me. They couldn't make choices for me but they could certainly nudge me in the right direction of my intended soul mate and
soul purpose!

And now, after thousands of readings as a psychic medium, I can
tell you that every spirit I have ever spoken to since has validated
what Kali told me in one way or another. I'm not the only one who has
been graced by this network of divine assistance. I have seen up close
and personal that not only do we get help from our immediate and
extended soul groups here on earth, and from spirit guides, angels,
master guides, and ascended masters in heaven, but as my show *The
Haunting Of . . .* provides evidence, some of us also get help from
chance encounters with trapped souls hovering between heaven and
earth—even if it comes to us in a roundabout way.

Consider what happened to actor, writer, and comedian Tom
Green. If you saw his episode of the show, then you know he was so
doubtful that there are really spirits that he set out during his college days to write a news article debunking stories that a museum
near campus was haunted. Of course his research, which included
a "night at the museum," took some unexpected twists and turns.
While we made many discoveries together upon returning to the
scene of his paranormal experience, the part of Tom's haunting that
has stayed with me since then was the revelation that the do-gooder
spirit Tom encountered during his college days actually stayed with
him for a long time afterward. I hope you didn't miss Tom's brief
mention of surviving a terrible accident many years and many miles
later while in Costa Rica because of the help of someone who came
to his aid, seemingly from out of nowhere. Did a soul who remained
on this plane because he took his role of providing security to

others so seriously send aid to Tom when he needed it most? Could Tom have been touched by a guardian angel on the beach that day? Hearing repeated stories such as his is what confirms for me what Kali has told me—that we are definitely not alone. We really can be given so much help in this life if we remain open to it.

Chapter 6

What Happens in Heaven

> *Lessons Learned There Don't Have to Stay There*

AS YOU KNOW BY now, I always had a strange relationship with the wee hours of the morning. Even though I hadn't heard a peep from earthbound souls in a long time, I still couldn't get a full night's sleep during my child-birthing years. When my eldest son, Nicholas, was born, he had such a terrible case of colic that he cried 24/7 for almost the whole first year of his life. There was nothing Anthony or I could do to console him. If Nicholas was up late, I was up too.

It took a visit from my aunt Irene to help relieve Nicholas's pain. You will recall that Aunt Irene was my father's sister—the one who spoke to angels in her sleep when she was a young girl. As the years passed we heard amazing stories about the medical miracles she was performing. One that was well documented was the healing of her son Daniel. After badly injuring his leg in a motorcycle accident, gangrene set in. When the doctors determined that all they could do was amputate the limb, he called my aunt and she rushed to be with him. My cousin was sleeping and heavily medicated by the time she arrived, but he woke up feeling as if several people were tugging on his leg, pulling it in all different directions at once. When he saw his mother standing at his bedside he said, "Ma, what are you doing?" He thought she was the one causing his excruciating pain. Of course she was, though she hadn't laid a finger on him. Apparently she called special *spirit* doctors together to perform some kind of surgery right then and there. She told Daniel that although he couldn't see these spirits, they were the ones manipulating his muscles and blood vessels in an effort to get all the poison out. The next morning her story proved to be true. The doctors at the hospital were stunned by my cousin's overnight recovery. There were no traces of gangrene, nor were there any explanations in their minds for how it disappeared.

When Aunt Irene was staying with us and she heard the pain my son Nicholas was in due to his colic, she asked me if it was okay for her to help him. Honestly, her ways were a mystery to me but I was delirious from lack of sleep and at the end of my rope. I thought, "If she was able to cure her son, maybe she can help mine," so I gave her permission. After she told my mother and me to leave the room, I peeked through the half-open door and watched apprehensively as she began praying intently over Nicholas's head. After a good five minutes, the screaming suddenly stopped. Done. Not a whimper. Not a sigh. Just silence. Do you know that Nicholas slept for two whole days after that, just as she said he would? She told us, "Don't even wake him up to feed him. Only do that if he stirs on his own." He clearly needed the sleep to replenish all the energy he spent while crying for months. To this day he is a sound sleeper. I am so grateful to her for her help.

Even though Nicholas's colic was cured, I remained a night owl. I guess it was just conditioning by then. Joseph was born; then came Anthony Jr. And despite having a houseful of boys who were up early every morning with boundless energy, I loved my conversations with Kali so much that I stayed up late many nights to continue talking with her. Our conversations helped put so much in perspective for me.

One of the more interesting talks we had was about what happens to the soul in the hours and days after our bodies die. Again, I believe she shared her perspective with me so that ultimately I could share it with the world, so here's what she had to say:

The Soul's Fascinating Journey After Death

In somewhat greater detail than I'll relate here, Kali told me that we ascend into the light with the assistance of our spirit guides. During this ascension a magnificent light bathes us and infuses us with megadoses of knowledge. As we approach the astral plane, loved ones who have gone before us greet us. There are many rooms in heaven. I was glad to hear this part because it was consistent with what Jesus told his disciples when he said in John 14:2, "In my Father's house there are many dwelling places. If it were not so, would I have told you that I go to prepare a place for you?"

Kali then told me that we are ushered to one of these rooms according to our needs. Souls who have experienced deep trauma due to an extended illness or a violent death can be spiritually scarred by their experiences. These souls will often go to a resting place where they can remain until they rebound. Think of it as a soul infirmary.

Bear in mind that even after a soul heals from the trauma of that lifetime it will carry the memory of that trauma into all subsequent lifetimes. The soul is imprinted with every memory of every lifetime, carrying with it the wisdom of its ages.

If our soul is intact when we arrive in heaven, we progress to a room where we are made aware of the thoughts, emotions, and feelings related to us of everyone we've ever encountered in the lifetime we just departed. That's right, we will feel the impact of our every word, action, or thought the same way these other people have felt them—good or bad. At first I didn't understand this, but then Kali reminded me that there is no concept of time or space in this other dimension, so one can absorb and process a lifetime's worth of messages in an instant. I kind of imagine it like speed-reading through your own Akashic records.

Talk about an intervention! There is no way to leave this experience without a fair and honest assessment of what our soul needs to work on more. It will all come down to *What did your soul gain in this recent lifetime? Did you gravitate toward fear? Or did you get closer to love?* Because love is Enlightenment, the end goal is to learn how to love unconditionally without judgment and without ego. By using our newly developed Enlightenment, we inherently have the understanding that we need in order to contribute back to the greater good of all—*to love thy neighbor as thyself*—because we are all connected by a cosmic DNA. We all come from the same source, the same light.

By collaborating with a panel of elder souls who review these events with us, we can determine what our next soul-enhancing mission will be: Are we to serve as a spirit guide to others still on earth struggling with the same issues we struggled with and did not necessarily master, so that in helping others we are learning too? Or are we to rest until a new soul group is formed and we can return to earth to tackle our particular set of life lessons and goals again, hopefully with greater success?

Kali also explained that when we return to earth the next time we not only pick the members of our soul group we wish to live with and the lessons we are to focus on, as she mentioned earlier, but also pick where we will live, what our socioeconomic status will be, and many other relevant details.

TRYING TO COMPREHEND IT ALL

This last part of Kali's lesson made me pause for a bit because, as I've told you, I am a really skeptical person. I had to break it down to fully understand it. I could see why I would pick *my* family. We had so much fun together, especially when I was growing up. Our home was filled with lots of joy. In many ways we were living the American dream. My father and mother were upwardly mobile. They were determined to build a better life for us than they'd had, which they did. They improved our circumstances with every successive move they made, giving us so many advantages educationally, spiritually, and physically. But could the same be said for my husband, who we learned was placed in foster care immediately after he was born?

Anthony had such a tough road to travel that it's almost hard to imagine that he would have actively chosen his early life—or any of the secrets that surrounded it until he was an adult. I was there with him every step of the way as he searched for his birth mother and discovered the details of his adoption. He's generously allowed me to share that story here because it illustrates a number of important life lessons.

According to the agency records, his birth mom had suffered a great trauma when she was very young, and underwent electroshock treatments as a result. The evening we met her, she had a confused look on her face. She wasn't sure who we were or how we found her. She was living in a home for women who needed help getting on their feet—one with a shared bathroom and kitchen and with a landlord who was extremely protective of her tenants' privacy and well-being. All incoming calls were screened by this landlord, so it was hard to even confirm that we had the right place, but we persisted until she finally put our call through and we could arrange to visit. When Anthony and I arrived, we took his birth mother out for coffee and a hot meal. We were going to have a difficult conversation with her so we wanted her to feel as comfortable as possible. When she finally spoke, her first words were "I hope you don't think I did the wrong thing. I only did what I thought was best for you. If I had kept you, you would have been a human punching bag. I did it to try to give you a better life and I really hope you had a better one than I could have given you."

At first it *was* a better life. Anthony's foster parents were kind people who cared for him and gave him a name, an identity, and a loving home. But in those days if you had your own biological children you were not allowed to adopt. You could only care for a child until a more permanent home could be found. When Anthony was two years old the agency located that permanent home. He left the family he had grown to love so he could move in with a new one. Soon he was calling another woman "Mommy." He also had to adjust to the change of his own name. Instead of being called Joseph, which is what he had been called since birth, he was now forced to answer to the name of Anthony. When my in-laws brought him home, they placed him in a bedroom located on the third floor. It was separated from all the other rooms and had very limited light. He spent many nights in the dark crying for the only mommy he knew—his foster mother. His adoptive mother's attentions were just too divided, especially as the family grew. All of his siblings had difficult starts to life as well. One even suffered physically from the complications of juvenile diabetes. Another sibling, like Anthony, lived for many years not knowing she was adopted. To say that their home was filled with pent-up pain and emotional angst is an understatement. Although Anthony was a genuinely good kid, by the time he was seventeen his parents asked him to leave and gave him the lamest excuses as to why they thought it would be a good idea. He had no place to go, so he lived in his car for a while. He later found out the real reason. It was so another sibling could move back home—his parents needed the extra bedroom.

Sure, many people survive tough circumstances like Anthony's, but I just couldn't wrap my mind around why someone would actually choose such circumstances.

The more I thought about where his life went from there, the more it began to make sense to me. I started to analyze the soul group he was currently surrounded by. We were all people he chose as well. And I thought about how he got from that jumping-off point to here. That led me to wonder about the lessons he may have learned in heaven during the review of his last life.

I started to see a pattern in his present life and wondered if he actually agreed to this theme of abandonment. I asked Kali, "What if on some level he signed on to this so he could learn something of greater value from the experience? What if, like so many other people who feel repeatedly abandoned, he needed to realize that the love he's searching for is not within other people—but it's within himself?" Seeking it in others is *not* how he'll find his soul mission or how he'll find self-love. "What if this was just a huge lesson in learning how to nurture himself?" Once we love ourselves we tend to attract people into our fate who will love and nurture us as well. It's just the law of attraction. Kali encouraged me, so I suspected I was on the right track.

My wheels were really turning now. Adoption seems to be prevalent in my family, so my thoughts ran to the example of two cousins on my mother's side of the family. When my aunt was unable to have children she adopted two little girls—one was from Bogotá, Colombia, and the other from Florida. These two girls couldn't be more different, but they formed the most beautiful connection in this lifetime. They are so close that you realize not only why they were drawn to the same household but that, for better (as in this case) or worse, the biological way a soul gets here really doesn't mean anything. I began to think that maybe Anthony's birth mother was just a vehicle to get him here. That maybe *her* mission in this incarnation was simply to experience creation or childbirth. For whatever reason, maybe she was concerned that she wasn't capable enough or wouldn't have the means to support him for the better part of his lifetime, so her soul engaged in some kind of agreement with Anthony and his birth father to take him as far into his journey as she could. Maybe she just said, "Well, I'll get you there, but that's all I can really do for you, buddy."

As for his adoptive mother, I truly believe that she was supposed to learn unconditional love in this lifetime and it was these particular children who stepped up and agreed to teach it to her, which brings me to two important points about these lessons from heaven:

The first point is that *we really are all one family*—we come from the Divine Source, who is our ultimate parent, so our earthly parents can be chosen for who they are and what wisdom they can potentially impart, or they can be chosen just to get us here. Because we set our own soul mission with the help of heavenly counsel, our purpose for being here is spiritually divined rather than genetically determined.

When you understand this it becomes easier to avoid the whole vic-tim mentality and the nitty-gritty of asking "Why me?" If that question rings in your head, just dig deep and ask instead, "Why *did* I make this choice before coming here? What is it supposed to teach me? What am I to learn from all of this?" The good news is once we learn the lesson, we can move on to the next one. It is in the learning that we find our true freedom to move forward.

The second point is that as much as you may believe you are here to teach your children, the soul is ageless, so there is a very real pos-sibility that your children have joined your soul group to teach *you*. I didn't have to learn this from Kali. I've witnessed this countless times in readings.

This is especially true of kids who defy the norm in any way. For example, children with learning differences, health challenges, or dif-ferent sexual orientation are often born into their families to teach their parents valuable lessons about acceptance and unconditional love. These souls are the ones that usually teach parents to let go of their preconceived notions about what and who their children "should be" in order to fit in to society. Many of these children are more evolved souls whose mission is actually to be a teaching soul.

THE PERSUASIVE POWER OF KIDS

I really love when during my readings I encounter children waiting to be born. Witnessing how siblings figure out their birth order is a unique pleasure and honor for me. When I read for a woman who is going to have a baby I will often see the negotiation that went on between the different souls who are destined to be her children. For example, if there's a boy and a girl who have each picked her as a mother, they'll both hover around at the time of conception and talk about whose turn it is. They'll look at each other and say, "You want to go first? Or do you want me to?" I've seen this happen more than you know.

Sometimes I'll watch two souls decide that they are coming together. I can't always be sure if they are going as true twins or if they will follow each other within a year the way "Irish twins" do. These two have made a soul pact because they feel that they need to live this life as a unit, not as an individual soul. They are either coming to help each other or to provide double the support for the family. They don't want to be without each other, often because they believe they can accomplish their mission better as a united pair.

On occasion one of these children will back out, but they will always find a way to be with you. I know this from personal experience. Way before I ever became pregnant I said to my mother, "Ma, if I have a son at some point that's great, but I can't see myself living my whole life without having at least one daughter." My mother wasn't so sure about that. "I don't know, Kim. I don't see you having any daughters." Now remember, my mother had some psychic tendencies too, so I had to be sure. "Are you kidding? I was born to have daughters. My soul *needs* a daughter!" Not because I want to dress her up all frilly-frilly. It's just that I felt I wouldn't be complete unless I had a daughter. Perhaps it was that I wanted to have that close bond with her that I had with my mom. Then of course I had my sons Nicholas and Joseph. By my third pregnancy I was convinced this was it. I was having a girl. Anthony and I decided that although we'd talked about having four children, this would be our last one. We had a big mortgage and he was already working two jobs at the time, so supporting a family of just three children seemed more manageable. I was a little over five months into my term when I went for blood tests and the doctor said to me, "Kim, you'll have to come back for a sonogram. Don't get panicky. This is very common. Your blood tests are not where we want them to be. Lots of times we have readings that come back incorrect, so we're just playing it safe and double-checking." When I went for the sonogram, the technician spent a long time looking at the screen. After she left the room, I said to my husband, "Something's wrong. Either the baby's dead or there's a serious complication." Anthony was shocked. "What makes you say that?" Sure enough, my intuition was right. My baby had passed away two weeks earlier. We had no way of knowing its gender, because when a baby dies in utero its genitals shrink back inside its body. After the procedure I fell into a deep depression. I was in mourning. I couldn't sleep at night, so I stayed on the couch where I wouldn't disturb Anthony. It was the most devastating time in my life. During my follow-up appointment after the extraction, my doctor told me, "Kim, good news—you're pregnant again." I was dumbfounded. Whereas I can tell you the date and time I conceived my other children, I can't tell you with this one because it's still a mystery to me. PS: My youngest boy was born nine months later. Anthony Jr. came out with his fists held in front of his face as if he was fighting the world to get out. He was ten pounds, two ounces, and an absolute clone of my husband.

Now what I must tell you is that every psychic I have ever gone to after his birth talks about my daughter—some of them speak about her as if she's living. I usually don't interrupt them because I want to hear what they have to say. I asked the first of these psychics what this daughter looks like and was stunned to hear her described as having long black hair, high cheekbones, and olive skin. That's exactly how I've always pictured her—as looking like the perfect combination of my husband and me. But the most amazing thing was when I asked about her name, I was told, "It's Alexandria." That was it. I was speechless. I started hysterically crying. Although I am a medium too, and I really shouldn't have been so surprised.

"I want to know how you know that," I said. "My baby died. I don't have a daughter, but I always knew it was a girl and that was what her name was going to be. I've loved that name forever." That's when the psychic said, "Kim, you know how I know. You do have a girl, and this is how I see her."

Invariably every psychic, including this one, has told me that my daughter is deeply connected to my youngest son—"the son with the initial A." I can picture exactly what happened. Two souls found out that after Mommy's third baby there are no more entry points. One said to the other, "Listen, I'm going in. You need to sit this one out. You want to hang in the background and help us, you can. But I'm going in and that's just how it is." I'm convinced this is the way Anthony Jr. came to be my son and how Alexandria's soul got kicked out . . . or I should say, how she graciously backed off, because free will exists and is exercised on the other side of the veil as well as on this side.

If all this sounds crazy to you, it would help to know my son

Anthony. When he came out with both fists positioned for a round-house punch, we joked that we either needed a college fund because he was going to be an attorney or we were going to enjoy a big pay-day when he became a welterweight champion. From the minute this kid started talking, everything was his way or no way. And he's not just a determined soul; he's an old soul. He may have even played the seniority card with Alexandria, as he is clearly the dominant soul. Even when he was little he used words from a different era. I once asked him how he knew a certain phrase that seemed really out of charac-ter for a five-year-old child and he said, "What do you mean how do I know that? This is not the first time I was born you know." When I pressed to find out more, he said, "Remember when I was a big man?" Anthony Jr. has always been someone who knows what he needs, and apparently he needed to be here now. But despite the fact that he cut in line, Alexandria's soul still seems very attached to him. She backed out to give him life, and if I am to believe the readings I've had and the feelings I get whenever I think about them, she still watches over him. As that first psychic told me, Anthony Jr. has a spirit guide and it's his sister.

What is he in my life to teach me? Among the many lessons he's shared so far, one that seems perfectly suited to mention in this book is that he reminds me all the time to be more fearless.

SOUL CONTRACTS:
LIFE SENTENCE OR LIFE-CHANGING

There are other examples of choices souls make as part of their contract that appear confusing but which may serve a less obvious purpose in their soul's long-term growth. For instance, many people who stand on the outside looking in at difficult or strained relationships may wonder why anyone would pick those circumstances in advance. As a result of my conversations with Kali, all I can say is that we simply may not be aware of the terms of their contract and what they came here this time around to work on. Although I do not like to see people struggle or exist in anything other than the most optimal circumstances, perhaps one person changed the life of the other for the better in another lifetime, and the recipient of their good deed agreed to spend a part of this lifetime in their company as a means of giving back. The rationale might be as simple as "I'm going to learn patience, empathy, and the art of measuring my words in our time together while you learn the same from watching me." In cases like this, when a loved one seems unwilling to walk away from a failed relationship with a boss, roommate, friend, or spouse, you can make one last-ditch effort to get him to examine his reasons for toughing it out. You can encourage him to look honestly at his motivations. Is the relationship still somehow serving to help him or the other person grow despite its many challenges? Or is this person extending his contract well past his obligation date because he is afraid of taking that next step into the unknown? If, after exploring these possibilities together, this person remains firmly rooted in the relationship, it is a sure sign that he is not ready to break his contract yet. You can continue to state your feelings as best you can, but if these two people's mutual contract is not up, you can talk until you're blue in the face. It isn't likely to matter. Those two souls need to work on their goals for a certain amount of time until at least one of them understands what the lesson is and is ready to move on to the next. It can be very hard for others to watch this uncomfortable dance, but unfortunately it's not over till it's over, or as they say, until the fat lady sings. Well, you get what I mean.

Some of you reading about Alexandria's decision to end her soul contract prematurely so Anthony Jr. could join us may also wonder about people in your own life who either backed out or agreed by contract to live a short life. These are very difficult deaths to reconcile. It is never easy for a parent to lose a child. In the order of things, parents are supposed to die before their children. *The Haunting Of . . .* episode with Vince Neil speaks to that point eloquently. Here is a man who loved his daughter with his whole heart. It is hard to understand why she had to die so young. Maybe only she and her spirit guides will ever know. But clearly, in her short time on earth her life made a great impact. Love is the greatest gift one can give and receive, and it felt to me on that visit with him that they gave each other a lot of love, and still do. I trust that she is serving as a guardian angel, helping him fulfill his earthly mission. She is with him all the time in spirit and continues to watch over him until they can meet again.

Another early end to the soul contract that many people have a hard time understanding is suicide. What I've gathered from readings is that this is a very different type of ending to a contract. Many people who've taken their own life because of depression or because of conditions such as bipolar disorder have come through to tell me, "I am not being held accountable for this suicide." They have explained that it is viewed much the same way as someone who died of cancer because they didn't undergo chemo—either they didn't know the right remedy, it didn't come to them in time, or their death was caused by an imbalance in their body beyond their control. I often wonder if these imbalances were written into their soul agreement along with different possible ways to overcome such challenges. I guess for some, the pain is too much to bear, and I wonder again if their choice of exiting prematurely was also written into their contract. Although I have asked these questions, the answers are not always clear, as there is a fine line between what is predetermined before the birth process and what free will leads one to do in the moment at hand. I've come to accept that I may never know some things until I arrive on the other side again myself. However, every soul I've ever encountered from the other side who chose their own death to consciously avoid doing their soul work has told me the same thing and that is "I regret doing what I did and if I could, I'd take it back." In these instances, they all consistently say the emotional issues they dealt with on earth followed them into the afterlife. There is no escaping it and there is no easy way out. Plain and simple, we all have to do the work.

There is one reading I did with the mom of a teen who committed suicide that I will never forget because it illustrates this point well. This woman's daughter made a pact with her boyfriend. He had a terminal illness he did not want to suffer through, and she did not want to be without him for the rest of her lifetime. So the two of them decided to kill themselves together. What the daughter told me during the reading is that she should never have done that. While this was her boyfriend's soul exit point, it was never intended to be hers. She broke her contract out of codependency. As it turns out, she is not with him anyway. When her mother asked, "Why not?" she said, "Because we had two different paths on earth and two different paths in heaven. His exit point was written into his chart, so he moved on to where he was supposed to be. But the exit point I took wasn't written into mine." She explained that now she has to make it right. She described that process as a little bit like taking an intensive course in school. She said she had to double up on her lessons. The questions she faced at that point were "Do I return to earth right away?" or "Do I learn the lesson from this world?" But one thing she said she did realize was that he was holding her back from learning her lessons: "Perhaps that's one of the reasons he needed to exit. But I needed to learn how to be independent, and I decided I wasn't going to be. I was going to take the ride along with him." Spirit told her, "One of the reasons he needed to leave was so your soul could grow. You didn't grow but now you're going to have to grow another way." It's very likely she chose to become a guide for someone else who is struggling with the issue of codependency and that is how she is learning.

As you can see, the soul contract is probably the most important agreement each of us will ever have to comply with.

Determining Which End of the Agreement You're On

I don't know how you can read this chapter and not look around at the people in your life to figure out what purpose each one serves—how each one can help you fulfill your own life goals or how you can help them fulfill theirs. It's instinctive. It's human nature. Here is a little exercise to help you reflect on these questions. It is *not* designed to help you keep score. Hopefully it will open up a new and better channel of communication with the people you interact with all the time so each of you can stay on point in life. It may even bring about a new appreciation for the times when these folks challenge you most, as they just may be doing their job! This exercise could take several days of observation and thought on your part, but I believe it is well worth doing.

Make a list of every significant person in your life.

- Begin with those in your birth family—your parents, grandparents, and siblings. Add stepparents and stepsiblings or adoptive siblings if they apply.
- Now think about your partner or spouse, and your children or grandchildren if you have any. Even your in-laws—your parents-in-law, your brothers- and sisters-in-law, as well as your sons- and daughters-in-law—should appear on the list.
- Include your exes, their new spouses if they are involved in co-parenting or you have ongoing dealings with them, and stepchildren if there are any.
- And certainly add close friends, past and present.
- Neighbors, colleagues, bosses, teachers, clergy, or mentors who have made an impression as they pass through your life have a place on this list too.
- Also be sure to include any influence, positive or negative, that may not fall easily into one of these categories.

In a column next to each name, write some adjectives that best describe your relationship. If they were unusual, note the circumstances under which you met. Was the connection instant? Was it a slow build? Did you have to earn each other's trust?

Next to that, note what each person's energy is like. What emotions did each of these people elicit when you met? What emotions do they elicit now? Did the relationship evolve? Or have these people been a consistent rock for you? If the relationship evolved, how have each of you grown? If it's been steady, what are the traits you most consistently rely on?

If they push your buttons, ruffle your feathers, or press on your last nerve, reflect on what it is that they say or do that triggers this response. Does the trigger imply something more about you or them? Think carefully on this one, as they may be showing you the very issue you or they are here to work on.

In the last two columns, indicate all the things of importance they have done for you, and all the things of importance you have done for them. What are their expectations of you versus yours of them? Is the offer of help from any one of them fulfilling your needs more, their needs more, or both of your needs? *Again, bear in mind that this is* not *a scorecard. I do* not *believe in conditional love.* But this is a means of sorting out who is in your life to help you further your mission and who in your life needs your help to further theirs. Of course, there will be some people who are in your life for both purposes. You are together for mutual benefit. Remember to be as honest with yourself as you can be. It's very hard to stay objective when you are taking inventory of the people in your life and how they treat you. If you are someone who often feels as if you are the victim of other people's motives and actions, you may want to ask a trusted friend or family member who knows all the players to review your list with you for added perspective.

When this chart is completed you should begin to see patterns that can potentially increase your sensitivity to and understanding of your own life mission as well the mission of those around you. When you look at the give and take in your life, even when it's lopsided, you can determine where to redouble your efforts. You can see ways to maximize each relationship so all of you are fulfilling your larger purpose in life. This is a very commonsense approach to developing an intuition about the people around you. Like all of intuition, it is based in observing with your heart as well as your other senses. We don't always take the time to do this every day, but doing it every once in a while can help keep all our souls on track.

Part 2

For All Practical Purposes

Chapter 7

Coming to Your Senses

> The Many Different Ways Spirits Communicate

SOMETIME AFTER ANTHONY JR.'s first birthday, it was as if a dam broke. The floodgates crashed open, and the waves of spirits were back again. This time they were stronger than ever.

If my theory is correct, my guides kept them away long enough for me to meet one of the terms of my soul contract, which was to establish a family. Word must have gotten out that I'd had my last child and was no longer planning on having any others. That meant I was ready to begin the other part of my soul mission, which I had agreed to before I was born. I was ready to be the go-between, the voice for the spirit world. Instantly the ghosts were on me to get messages through to their loved ones. But apparently, this wasn't the only thing that invited them back in. There were several events leading up to this one that played a part too.

WHEN THE STUDENT IS READY,
THE TEACHER WILL APPEAR

I must give credit where credit is due, or—as I joked at the time—blame where blame is due. My sister, Sue, was friends with a woman named Katie who ran psychic fairs at a local martial arts dojo in the evenings. They met because Sue's husband was a black belt in karate and Katie's husband owned the dojo. One day Sue called me up and asked, "What are you doing tonight?" I said, "Nothing, why?" She told me to get Anthony to babysit the kids because Katie was having another one of her events and she thought it would be fun for us to go together and get a reading. It was early enough in the evening, so I thought, "What do I have to lose?" When we walked in, we were handed a mailing list for each of us to add our name, address, phone number, e-mail address, and so on to. Then we sat down and listened to this woman talk for about forty minutes. She was a psychic. Her name was Holly Chalnick, and I thought what she had to say was fascinating. She started speaking to spirits only after her sister passed away. It was her sister who led her from the other side of the veil to begin helping people here through readings. Although she certainly kept my attention, I wondered when the other psychics were coming. After the lecture ended, it was apparent that this talk was all that Katie had planned for the evening. There would be no readings—my sister misunderstood what Katie had said. But it was no big deal. I thoroughly enjoyed the talk, and although her story was sad, I genuinely liked Holly. I figured that the next time Katie had a psychic fair maybe Holly would be there and we could get a reading from her then. I went home. Done. Never thought about it again.

Two to three weeks later I got a phone call from Holly. And this is how the call went:

"Hi, Kim." (She had a very soft voice.) "This is Holly Chalnick."

"Hi, Holly. How are you?"

"You attended one of my seminars recently and you signed a mailing list."

"Yes, I really enjoyed your lecture that evening. It was very nice."

"Well, I just want to tell you the reason I'm calling. It's because I was going through my list and something jumped out at me when I came to your name."

"What do you mean?"

"Well, I just want to tell you you're very psychic."

I was surprised to hear her say this. "I never really even met you," I said.

She laughed. "I know but you didn't need to meet me. I picked that up from your handwriting and the vibrations of your name. My spirit guides told me that I needed to call you. I give classes on development."

Now the skeptical, cynical person that I am was thinking, "What a crock of shit this is. This lady is trying to get people for her class. She's just going down the list and calling us one by one." Well, I'm no dummy. There was no way I was going to tell her I even suspected she might be right. But of course I continued to be nice and cordial. "Oh, wow, that's really interesting. It's so weird that you would even know that."

"Oh yes," she insisted. "You definitely do. Listen, I live just one town over from you, so the class is close enough for you to just try it."

Now I'm really thinking this is a setup.

I asked, "When are your classes?"

"I hold them in the mornings on Tuesdays and Thursdays."

Great. I had the perfect out. "Oh, Holly, I'm the sole caregiver to my youngest son." (My eldest boy was in grade school, my middle child was in pre-K for half the day, and the baby was home with me.) "I'm a stay-at-home mom so I couldn't possibly take your class."

"Oh, what a shame. That's terrible. You're so gifted, my dear. You're so gifted."

"I don't know what to tell you, Holly, but thanks for thinking of me."

"Okay, but if anything should change, let me know. I'm not going to forget you."

I was thinking, "Ah, geez," but I ended the call with a polite "thank you" and that was that.

As soon as I got off the phone, I called my sister and left a message on her voice mail: "That lady Holly from the psychic lecture a few weeks ago is going to call you. She's trying to solicit people for her class. I just want to give you the heads-up. I don't know if you want to go, but it really doesn't sound too kosher to me. She's a teacher and she's trying to find some paying students. I told her no, thanks, but do what you want to do."

One day went by; two days went by; a week went by; two weeks went by. Holly never called my sister. Finally, a year went by and my phone rang.

"Hi, Kim. This is Holly again. I told you I won't forget you."

(In all that time I never went for a reading with her and never followed up on her offer to take the class. Nothing. I had no other communication with her at all.)

"Hi, Holly. It's been a while since I heard from you. How are things?"

"Well, I have good news for you."

"You do?"

"Guess what? I'm giving night classes now so don't tell me that you can't find a babysitter. I'd love you to come join us. Can your husband watch the kids? It's only an hour and a half—two hours tops. I just want you to try it."

I reluctantly said, "All right, tell me about your class. How does this work?"

"Well, it's held at my house. There's going to be about twelve other people there too, and I'm going to teach you how to develop your intuition. I'm going to recommend a lot of books for you to read and we're going to do a lot of exercises together. You know, psychic exercises."

"How much will this cost?"

She told me the fee and then she added, "I do, however, request that you pay for it in full before the first class."

I said, "Holly, I have to tell you that's where I have a problem. I wouldn't feel comfortable paying for your course in full if I'm not sure I'm going to like it. I'm just being honest with you. I'm going to take your advice and I'll take the class, but I'd like to pay as I go if that's okay with you?"

(You'll remember that I learned a long time ago that sometimes you just have to step up your boundaries a notch. I felt, given this woman's persistence, this was one of those times.)

She caved in. "Okay, you know what? I'm going to honor that request because that's how strongly I feel you should be in my class."

There were twelve sessions in all, and once a month there was an additional get-together where the students from her other classes met to practice reading each other. Those were free and they were optional.

When I showed up for the first session I still had my doubts. I really didn't know what to expect from this course. Were we going to be cutting the heads off chickens? Or doing even crazier things than that? This world was still a big mystery to me. How could I be sure this wasn't just hocus-pocus? Some form of magic? Most of all, I wondered how mediums knew what they knew. But I gave in because my curiosity got the better of me, and I could also tell this woman was not going to give up any time soon.

When Holly asked if anyone had questions, my hand was the first in the air. Mainly, I wanted to know how this all fit into my religious beliefs. It was still my most nagging concern. But Holly's smart answer helped make more of a believer out of me. She said, "This is all about *energy;* not necessarily about religion. Psychics come from all different denominations. This practice doesn't have anything to do with that. It has to do with your *energy system.* It's like learning to read a book, but instead you're learning to read energies—your own and others'. You'll also learn how that energy fuels your intuition and the many senses associated with it."

I instantly loved her teaching style. I appreciated how she explained things so they made sense to me and the other students. Everything she was saying was in line with what I already thought. I believed in the power of intuition, so I was beginning to really warm up to the idea of this class.

One week she was teaching us about the power of crystals. The next week she was teaching us more about chakras—the system she was referring to that draws energy to us and not only circulates it within our bodies but emits it in the form of auras. The week after that she delved into spirit guides. She taught us about psychometry, which is when you hold an object to feel its vibrations so you can get a reading from it. There were other modalities she explored with us too. I was learning so much.

One thing I kept being drawn to was the subject of past-life regressions. It was in this class that I first got interested in it. Holly gave us this whole list of books to read and I devoured them all. I particularly liked *Many Lives, Many Masters* by Dr. Brian Weiss because this guy was the farthest thing from a quack. I was really attracted to the authors who were serious, thoughtful, and educated practitioners. I only wanted to be associated with this field if it was for real. I'd have no interest in it if it were populated with only kooky people and kookier ideas. Dr. Weiss studied at Columbia University and graduated from Yale University's School of Medicine. He was head of psychiatry at the Mount Sinai Medical Center. It doesn't get more real or prestigious than that. When one of his patients began discussing past-life experiences with him while she was under hypnosis, he didn't dismiss what she revealed to him as improbable or as a figment of her imagination. Instead he used his curiosity to find out more about the prospect of reincarnation. He probed and explored until he could confirm parts of her story through public records, historical documents, and books. This research verified the facts she'd spoken about from the different time periods she'd lived in. He ultimately became convinced that what she was telling him was possible—that the human soul does survive death. I loved that he dug and dug until he could explain to himself what no one else could. I admired and respected that kind of investigation and openness to possibilities. It was when I read Dr. Weiss's book that I decided I wanted to explore more and perhaps become a past-life regressionist. I loved it, loved it, loved it.

By then, we were in our sixth week of class and every time one of those optional get-togethers came up Holly wouldn't take no for an answer. She kept telling me that I was her best student, even though I had never done a reading for anybody and even though all I wanted to do was focus on this other area of interest. I asked her point-blank, "How can you tell me I'm the best student you have?"

"It's the same way that I saw your name on a list and knew right away you should be in the class," she said firmly. "And why do you keep questioning what my gift is? My gift tells me that you're the best student here, you're going to be a well-known medium one day, and that you just need to trust me on this."

I shot back quickly, "I'm sorry, I can't just trust you on this, because I believe in the power of suggestion and I know how that goes." You wouldn't believe how frustrated this woman got with me. I knew I was being incredibly stubborn so I took the tone down a level. "With all due respect, I wouldn't be coming back to your class every week if I didn't find it fascinating, but you have to let me find my own truth. I really don't want to be a medium. I love this past-life regression stuff and this is what I want to do."

She laughed, "Let me tell you something, Kim. Not only are you going to be a medium, but your husband is going to build a room in your house and you're going to work from that room doing readings and giving people comfort. It's going to be a beautiful room." (PS: She was right!)

She had such a way with me. It was her soft voice, her laugh, and the quiet assurance with which she'd always say, "Okay, Kim. We'll see." It was nice. She really knew how to deal with me. I'm sure she'd encountered skeptics before but none quite like *this* resistant student.

WHEN THE TEACHER IS READY, THE STUDENTS WILL APPEAR

Holly was definitely a pivotal person in helping me get on the road to Enlightenment. I loved her classes and while not every lesson she taught resonated with my soul, I learned to take what I needed and to leave the rest. As I continued on my path, I discovered more and more. I was like a sponge, absorbing universal truths that touched me on a very deep level. I wasn't afraid to do the work, and the spirit world responded by teaching me directly. Many years later I was instructed by my spirit guides to create my own class. Of course, I made all types of excuses at first. "Where will I find the time?" I thought. "I'm not a teacher but I'm a very good student." Without skipping a beat, I heard clearly the words, "Please learn to trust us, as we will give you the lesson plan." I knew I needed to do this. It was important to offer others the same type of guidance that Holly once offered me, so I created a class called the Enchanted Circle. I also knew that I needed the right mixture of students to make the class work optimally, so I trusted that if my divine sources were giving me the lesson plan, they would also send me the students. One by one they filtered in—the perfect blend of energy from all walks of life and every age group. Once the class started, we instantly formed a spiritual bond, and some even called me *Sensei*.

Let me explain. Not only did my spirit guides provide the lesson plans and the students, but they provided the space too. I asked a friend if he knew of a place where I could teach my class, and he immediately connected me with a friend of his who is a karate instructor named Joe. Joe was over the moon to hear my request. In exchange for use of the space where he taught his classes, all he wanted was to be one of my students. It was a perfect match for all concerned. I later realized that I first met Holly at a dojo and now years later I was teaching a class at a dojo. The Universe sure has a way of conspiring to bring us what we need and, yes, the lesson plans kept coming. Each week I taught a different class, which was designed to be very hands-on. Although the class was intended to be a six-week course, it lasted one full year. I kept trying to gently push my students out of the nest when I thought they were ready, but their continued interest was completely unanimous. None of them wanted to leave. However, my goal was not to have for-ever students; my goal was to teach the man how to fish so he could satisfy his own spiritual hunger and in turn pay the blessing forward. And forward it has been paid. I am so proud to announce that most, if not all, of my loyal students are practicing and teaching what they have learned in one form or another. The following are just a few exercises that I taught them. I thought you might enjoy reading about them here and trying a few on your own. I picked exercises at this point that focus largely on increasing your *awareness* of the energy around you and that engage you in just playing with it a bit. We will have an opportunity later to expand on these exercises and use your energy more fully.

LESSONS FROM THE ENCHANTED CIRCLE

WHAT YOU SHOULD SAY AND DO BEFORE ANY PSYCHIC EXERCISES AND COMMUNICATION WITH SPIRIT

If you were an art student using the communal brushes and paints in the studio where you studied, you would clean the brushes first so the paint residue left behind by the previous artist didn't muddy the colors you planned to apply to your new canvas. The same is true when the material you are working with is energy. You have to clean the energy left in the room by those before you if you hope to achieve the best results. Holly had a favorite method for doing this, and just thinking about it makes me laugh. The first time I entered her home for class I thought, "I can't believe it. This chick's smoking pot." But I quickly learned that the strange scent I was smelling was burning sage. Sage, as I mentioned earlier, was used by Native Americans to help cleanse their space and call forth the souls of certain ancestors for protection. When the sage is lit, its smoke filters through the air releasing whatever negative energy is trapped in the crevices and corners of a room. Instead of using the smudge-stick variety, Holly preferred burning loose sage with a shell and an eagle feather because it came directly from the Native American tradition. That is how I use it too.

Sage is not only a good clearing agent, but also a good measure of what negative energy was present before. It's believed that the more smoke that comes from the sage, the more the space needed to be cleansed. Remember to open a window when you are burning sage because you really want whatever gets caught up in the smoke to leave your environment. It can be dangerous to stir up negative energy, bring it to the surface, and then just leave it there to attach itself to whoever enters the space afterward. As you are cleansing a room, you should always say a prayer. Again, I usually say a simple one such as,

"Only spirits of the light are welcome in this space. If you are not from the light, you need to leave now."

Although Holly was Jewish, she would also recite what Christians call the Lord's Prayer or the Our Father. Although I never asked her why she did this, I think the last lines of the prayer that request freedom from temptation and protection against evil said what she needed to say in the event dark forces emerged, so she simply borrowed from it the way she borrowed from Native American traditions.

Because burning sage removes negative energy, it also makes the air around you less dense, allowing you to raise your vibrations. Once in this elevated state, you can meditate on whatever you hope to achieve during your session, asking Spirit to help you achieve your purpose. In our case, the purpose was higher learning.

GETTING STARTED WITH PSYCHOMETRY

Sometimes it's hard to pick up on someone's energy right out of thin air. It can help to hold a personal item belonging to either the person you are reading for or the person they are trying to connect with, because we all leave an imprint of our energy on the things that we wear, use, or are around daily (much like the way we leave fingerprints on whatever we touch!). Examples of items that retain our energy include an article of clothing, a photo, or a piece of jewelry. Getting energetic impressions off objects like this is called psychometry. I taught this practice first because it's a great exercise for beginners. Holding the article in your hand provides a little help, while the results provide a little extra confidence. To try it for yourself, simply ask a friend if they can place in your hands something of theirs that is dear to them. As you hold this object, just relax and let whatever images, sounds, or feelings intended for you to come to you naturally. Don't think about them, doubt them, filter them, or anything. It's as if you are a dream catcher. Your mind is a web and it is receiving whatever small particles of information this object is floating into the air for you. Then tell your friend whatever you experienced. I promise you'll be amazed by their reaction, and by what you just did too.

USING THE ENERGY BALL TECHNIQUE

I loved watching the show *Bewitched* when I was a kid.

Remember when Esmeralda licked her finger and held it up in the air? It acted like a lightning rod, drawing energy to her. This may have been one of the first ways I subliminally learned about energy. This exercise helps create a strong awareness of the energy already surrounding you. You don't need to draw it from anywhere else. To create a field of energy from the chi already in your presence, start by rubbing your two hands together very quickly, the way you would on a cold winter day. Then pull your hands apart, paying attention to the resistance between them that you feel. Now shape this energy into a sphere the way you'd shape a snowball. Once this energy sphere is about the size of a baseball, place an intention inside of it through your thoughts. Some people keep it very basic at the beginning by thinking of a specific color and infusing it into the ball. When the creator of the energy ball sends it to the receiver by visually imagining it landing at one of the receiver's body parts, nine times out of ten, the receiver will not only feel that energy landing, but also be able to tell you what body part the creator of the ball aimed for and what color they were sending.

If you didn't believe that thought and intention attaches itself to energy before, you will definitely believe it now. This exercise not only raises your awareness of the energy around you, but teaches you the importance of controlling negative thoughts. It also teaches you that manifesting positive energy is totally within your grasp!

DEVELOPING YOUR SIXTH SENSE WITH THE ZENER CARD EXPERIMENT

This was one of the more popular exercises in class. It is widely used in psychic development and is designed to teach people extrasensory perception, or ESP. I developed my own deck of cards by placing images of shapes, colors, and objects on index cards. You can use a homemade deck like this or a deck of regular numbered playing cards. Both are effective. Sit back-to-back with a friend. Then alternate turns picking a card from the deck. When it's your turn, focus on the card's picture, sending it energetically to the other player. Really concentrate on the picture's details. Then ask the receiver to identify the object you were thinking about. You should both have some paper and a pen to record how many you get right. Again, your accuracy will surprise you.

ENGAGING IN REMOTE VIEWING

Trust me when I tell you we really do have the ability to travel outside of our physical bodies through the time-space continuum to clairvoyantly see and predict scenarios. I firmly believe anyone can be taught to do this. First you need to clear your mind. Then begin a guided meditation to help place you into a theta-wave state. This is the same state we go into when we are ready to fall asleep. It's when we are most relaxed and open.

When you are in this mind-set, you can project your psychic senses and observe scenes as close to you as in the next room or as far away as thousands of miles. Once you've projected your energy into the desired space, you can use your other psychic senses to identify objects there or to observe what is happening. This technique is commonly used by military personnel to see into an enemy camp and gather intelligence. Real-life psychic spies use this technique even today.

To test your own abilities, ask a friend or family member to place a very obscure object on a desk or a bookshelf in another room close to you. After meditating to call your energies into focus, project those energies into the other room and see if you can identify the object and locate where it was placed. Write down or draw what you are seeing. Sometimes you will envision the exact object. Other times you may draw its correct shape. And of course, there will be times when all you will get is the correct color. Remember, this is a process. Learning to do this well is a matter of developing one of your chakra centers known as the psychic third eye. We'll talk more about training the third eye in subsequent chapters. For now just know that enhancing that ability is no different than exercising your muscles for improved results. The more you flex those muscles, the stronger they become.

Those of you who watch my show will recall that I did one of these exercises with Chris McDonald and another with Richard Burgi in their respective episodes of *The Haunting Of . . .* Both were very surprised by what they picked up on. Of course, I wasn't. I knew they had these abilities all along!

My study and practice of remote viewing quickly led to a curiosity about how this ability helps people have precognitive experiences—in other words, how it enables them to see into the future. What I learned is not only strange but true. It confirmed that I had to think like a scientist, or as I prefer to say, like a "psychic investigative journalist." This was not magic we were doing. There was always an explanation if you pursued it far enough.

What I found out is that our souls are connected by a silver cord. It's an energetic lifeline that extends from a chakra point such as the Crown chakra at the top of your head, much like a spiritual umbilical cord, so that our soul can return to our body after we allow it to roam around a bit. The times when our soul most commonly wanders is when we are sleeping.

Many psychics see this cord when they are visiting people in hospice. They can visualize the cord getting thinner and thinner as the person nears death. They are actually witnessing the process of letting go. But while you are living, this cord tethers you to your body so you can peek into the other side of the veil and still safely return.

Maybe you've read about examples of this and didn't even realize it. Many people's souls tap into universal events while sleeping. For example, lots of people reported dreaming about 9/11 before it happened. These precognitive dreams, where you see things that haven't occurred yet, are possible because in other dimensions there is no time and space. If what constitutes the future is a timeline, then entering the other side where no such order exists allows you to glimpse these events in advance of when they will happen in our dimension.

Hopefully now you can see how my curious nature sucked me into the psychic world deeper and deeper. I was beginning to exist in my own little vortex, which I somehow got caught up in. The more I learned, the more I had to know!

WHAT YOU SHOULD SAY AND DO BEFORE ENDING THESE ENERGY EXPLORATIONS

Because psychics and mediums spend so much time operating at higher vibrations, they can be a little spacey. They have to make a conscious effort to return to their body after their work or study is done. Planting or rooting yourself back into your earthly body is called grounding yourself. There are many ways to do this. To practice the method we used in class, place your feet firmly on the floor, then visualize three energy cords (you may see them as bright pillars of light with tiny roots at the ends similar to roots on a tree) extending from the soles of your feet into the center of the earth. Once these roots have burrowed deep enough into the ground, imagine the ends of them securing you in place. Visualize one more energy cord with roots extending from your tailbone into the center of the earth. (Note: You may feel a slight tug in the area of your tailbone. This is quite normal.) Lastly, you should picture a white beam of light shooting up from your crown toward the sky so that you are not just firmly connected to the earth but also held by the positive power of the heavens. I also recommend that you close the session with a meditation thanking Spirit for what you have learned or experienced.

If you are taking a class and driving home afterward, it is especially important to take these steps for practical purposes as well as spiritual ones! You don't want your head in the clouds when you're in a vehicle on the road.

NO FAIR!

So I finally finished Holly's class. I was enjoying reading more about past-life regressions, and as you know, I was practicing this modality on my husband, Anthony. Holly's course taught me so much that I began to think she had cleared a special pathway of learning for me—it was around this time that I first met Anthony's spirit guide, Kali, during regressions. Since you are already well acquainted with Kali and her teachings, you can imagine how invigorating this whole period was for me. Life was good, very good.

Then one day, I got another unexpected call.

"Kim, it's Holly. Listen, sweetie. You know the Eyes of Learning in Hicksville?" (The Eyes of Learning is a spiritual center that still exists today. They host workshops and fairs relating to a wide variety of metaphysical topics. It's a great place to meet people and exchange ideas, talk about the latest books you've read, and discover other writers or practicing mediums to follow.)

"Well, they're hosting the next psychic fair and I'm going to be one of the readers," she continued. "They definitely need another reader, so I volunteered you."

"*What?!* No, Holly. No," I protested. "I'm sorry to disappoint you but I don't want to read. Please don't do this to me. I know how persistent you can be. I know you won't give up, but I'm begging you."

"Sweetie, you have to consider that this information does not come from you."

"I know that, Holly. I learned that from you. But I'm not confident. I'm not there yet. Please, please don't do this to me. I'm having anxiety just thinking about it. You don't know, but I won't be able to sleep between now and then." (It was just weeks away!)

"Oh my God, I didn't know you were going to have such a strong reaction. Okay, okay. I won't make you do it, but I'm telling you you're ready, and I'm telling you Spirit is going to show you you're ready."

"All right, when I'm ready I'll do it. Not before then, though. Okay? Do we have a deal?"

"Yes, we have a deal."

I hung up the phone thanking God that I got her off my back. It's not so easy saying no to this woman. But it was over now. Done. I could breathe again knowing I didn't have to go do this fair.

The fact that I was off the hook with Holly, however, didn't mean I was off the hook entirely. Other strange things were beginning to happen that were impossible to ignore. There was this one morning after a fabulous late-night session regressing Anthony when I was in my room making the bed. It was a beautiful sunny day. The baby was taking his morning nap, my husband was at work, and my two other boys were at school. I was arranging the last of the throw pillows against the headboard when I turned and saw a silhouette in the doorway. It was transparent and standing directly in my field of vision—not in my mind's eye. This wasn't a girl who just wandered into my house or a spirit conversing with me in my head. This was an actual visitation. I'd seen enough in my lifetime to know I was having a supernatural experience like the ones I had had when I was a child. But this time the visitor was a pretty girl about fourteen or fifteen years old. She had long dirty-blond hair. And she spoke to me. The immigrant ghosts, you'll remember, never said a peep. But this girl's words infiltrated my head. I didn't hear them out loud. I heard them internally, with the volume turned way up. She said, "I died in a fire. I'm from New Jersey. Please call my mom and dad and tell them I'm okay."

After pausing for a minute to take in what I had heard, I thought, "I don't even know this girl. How the hell am I going to find her mother and father? It'll be like finding a needle in a haystack." She not only heard my questions, but also responded. She told me their names and the town they were from. For the life of me I don't remember the information she relayed to me because as quickly as it came to me it left. I was so stunned by her appearance that I didn't think of those questions with the intention of receiving or doing anything with the answers. It was so surreal that my brain was too busy processing the how and why of it all to hold on to the other information.

Before anything else could be said, she turned to leave. I could see that the whole left side of her face was charred beyond recognition. It was something out of a horror movie. Then she just floated away. I remember standing there, noticing how light everything was around me. The sun was beaming into my room. It was an intense light, reminiscent of the rays from the street lamp that would cast a glow in my childhood room at night.

It had been a long time since I had seen a spirit physically right in front of me like that. I can still picture it to this day. It really freaked me out. My heart was beating, my adrenaline was pumping, and I couldn't help but wonder if when I put Anthony under hypnosis I had opened a channel that couldn't be closed. Or did taking Holly's class stir up unwanted visitors? "Did I invite this in again?" I was blaming myself. "What did I do? I did this. I know I did." It was like the Ouija board I had always been warned not to use. I kept thinking, "I never should have messed with this stuff."

THINGS ALWAYS COME IN THREES

At this point I was going to the library and the local bookstore regularly, reading everything I could get my hands on that spoke to my soul. I needed to understand what was happening to me. Back then it was not like it is today, where there are television shows and even whole cable networks devoted exclusively to metaphysical topics. I had to actively seek out the information I needed.

John Edward was already quite popular at the time. He had written several books by this point and also had a radio show on WPLJ. He was really drawing the public's attention to the world of psychic phenomena, along with a few other pioneering mediums of the day.

I was listening to his show one day when I decided to call in. I didn't think I could talk to him about my specific situation, but I thought, "Wouldn't it be hot stuff if I just got a chance to speak to him in general?" I dialed the number and heard the person on the other end of the line say, "WPLJ, hold on." I was so excited. While I was waiting my turn, John told the caller before me that her grandmother was coming through and she was showing him something that was familiar to him. He said, "Your grandmother is telling me that you once put a pin in an electrical outlet and it opened up something inside of your energy field."

This really got my attention. The woman said, "No, I didn't do that." But he continued, "Well, your grandmother's telling me that she watches you all the time. She's your biggest spirit guide and she's encouraging you. I don't know why she's showing me this. You didn't get electrocuted or anything when you were younger?" The lady said "No, no." She was bewildered. Meanwhile, I was thinking to myself, "Could this even be? I bet you that's *my* grandmother." I was on hold, I was probably the next caller in line, and I was almost 100 percent sure this message was for me.

There was an incident when I was five years old. It was Christmas Eve and my mother was cooking her traditional *frutti di mare* (aka the dinner of seven fishes). My aunt Patti was next door cooking her half of the meal because they always shared that chore. While they were getting things ready, we were all sent to play. My sister was at my cousin's house and I was sitting by myself on the couch next to our Christmas tree just down the hall from the kitchen. I remember it like it was yesterday. First I watched some TV. *The Munsters* was one of my favorite shows, and I loved *Batman* too. When both episodes were done, I spent time looking at all the ornaments on the tree. My mother used to give us each a special one every year. After that, I got on the floor to look at the nativity scene. She always made it look so nice with fresh cotton all around it like snow. I was thinking about Jesus, Mary, Joseph, and the wise men—the whole story of Christmas—when I saw a safety pin right next to an electrical socket. I was the kind of kid who asked so many questions my mother would just give up and say, "Because that's the way God wanted it." It seemed my curiosity could never be satisfied. I can't tell you why I felt the need to put the pin in the socket, except maybe just to see what would happen.

Naturally, when I did that I got electrocuted. I shot across the room. I'll never forget looking down and seeing that my whole arm had turned charcoal black. Huge chunks of it were scorched. There was no fire. Nothing like that—just this big streak of black. I went running to my mother, holding my arm up in the air and crying, "Mommy! Mommy!" Now you have to know that my mother was not exactly the calm type. When we got hurt she would freak out. That was my mother's downfall. She would always say, "If you choke I'm running the other way." That was truly her biggest fear. She could handle just about anything but a medical emergency.

She got so nervous that she started yelling at me, "What did you do?! What happened?" She was frantic, but she managed to take a dishcloth and wrap it around my arm before she and her sister, who also lived close by, raced me to the hospital. There the doctor applied Silvadene—a salve for healing bad burns—and bandaged the wound up really well. He told me it would take time to heal and warned me not to take the gauze off at all. He also said he couldn't guarantee that I wasn't going to have scars. Believe it or not, he did such a good job that my arm healed perfectly. To look at it today you would never know what happened.

Before I could tell John all about this, the show started winding down. I heard the producers say, "Okay, John. You were fabulous. Oh my God, that was amazing. That's all we have time for today. You can tune in to John next week at . . ." Seconds later, all I heard was a busy signal. The person on the other end had hung up. But that's not where the story ends.

That same week Katie called me and asked if I wanted to go to a book signing at Borders in Levittown. We had become really good friends since that first lecture Holly gave, and I was keeping her up to speed on the things happening in my life. She would always encourage me to develop my skills, and on that particular day she knew the subject of the book being signed would interest me. It was about life after life, so of course I said, "Oh my God, *yes,* I want to go." I had never heard of the author, but since Katie knew so many people in the psychic world I was happy to take her reading recommendations.

While we were in line waiting to meet the author, Katie saw someone she knew. "There's a friend of mine," she said. "Excuse me while I go say hello." A few minutes later she motioned me over to introduce us. "Kim, I want you to meet John Edward; John, this is my friend Kim. She's a fabulous up-and-coming medium." I looked at him and blurted out, "*You're John Edward?* I am so sorry, I thought you were so much older. I hear you on the radio all the time, but I didn't picture you to be so young." He smiled and admitted he heard that a lot. Then I launched right into what was on my mind. "John, I can't believe you're standing in front of me. Do you remember last week during the final reading on your show you told a woman that she put a pin in an electrical outlet and she didn't know what you were talking about? I was on hold waiting to get through but the show ended before I could. I think that message was for me." He put his hands up in the air and said, "Of course, it's for you." I wasn't sure what he meant, so he explained: "Every time I'm on the radio and there is a message that doesn't register with the person I'm telling it to I always get a letter or an e-mail from a listener telling me that the message was intended for them. This time I didn't get an e-mail from anyone, but now here you are validating it for me in person. Absolutely that message was for you."

Now wait, hold on. It gets even better. The very next day I'm in the library in the New Age section taking out as many books as I can. I didn't care if the book dated back to the 1920s. It was as if I couldn't feed my curiosity in this area enough. One book I picked up that day was called *The Link* by Matthew Manning. So what page do you think I opened up to? You guessed it. It was one on electrocution. In the introduction to this book, Peter Bander was relaying the results of a study carried out on a very small scale by a Dr. Joel Whitton. This is what he wrote: "A number of known psychics had been asked by Dr. Whitton to fill in a questionnaire. Their answers to questions about personal experiences during early childhood showed several of the psychics had one experience in common. . . . The common experience of the psychics was simply that they all had suffered a severe electric shock before the age of ten."

My jaw dropped. I must have reread that line ten times while standing there. It was really hard for me to ignore the series of coincidences that happened that week. The spirit world evidently wanted me to know this information. My guides and all my dead relatives were conspiring. They knew I wouldn't be satisfied until I understood why I had these strange abilities and why I was being called on to use them now. I'm still that way. If I don't understand something, I can't process it. When I finally comprehend it, though, I'm totally on board. In this instance, I couldn't shake the feeling that they were saying, "Let's just let this chick know why this happened so she can move on and complete her mission already." I can be that annoying. It's just the way I am. After all, I am a Gemini.

I left the library that afternoon feeling as if my grandmother was telling me, "Hey, Kim. You know what? I didn't have any idea about this stuff when I was alive, but I'm finding out about it over here. They're telling me that this is how this happened to you. They're saying, 'Remember that time when you were five and you did that thing with the safety pin and electrical socket? Well, here's proof of what triggered things.' First they sent you a message through the phone call to John Edward, then they confirmed it at the book signing, and finally they led you to a chapter in that book that spelled it all out for you."

Well, I don't need a brick to land on my head! I got it. Really, I got it. That had to be why a few years after that Christmas I was seeing ghosts at the foot of my bed. That was the event that opened up a portal for me—and if it didn't, it certainly enhanced my gifts!

So now here I am with a backstory and a better sense of history, but still no clue about how to turn off all the noise the spirits reappearing in my life were making. It was déjà vu all over again, but this time it was worse than in my childhood because it was happening every freakin' minute of the day and night, and now spirits were coming through to me using any and all of my senses. It was game on.

I was hardly a stranger to invasions of personal space, but I started to worry. If this was my new normal, just how abnormal was normal going to get?

Despite the chaos, I refused to tell Holly about any of this. I knew if I did she would tell me I was ready to read with her at the fair!

Just so you know, it would take years from this point on for Holly and my guides to teach me how to deal with and maximize each of the different types of spirit communications I was experiencing. I called those years my apprenticeship, but let me save you some time by giving you a speed course on these modes of communication, describing how they work for me now, after much trial and error. (In chapter 10 you will get a chance to be *my* apprentice, but more on that later.)

Meet My Friends the "Clairs"

The first "Clair" I'd like to introduce you to is *clairvoyance*. By *standard* definition, clairvoyance is when a medium experiences clear seeing. Since I was never one for doing things the typical way, and it's doubtful that all mediums experience it the same, I'll just tell you how it happens for me.

Most times when spirits are trying to communicate something to me visually (because that's the way they are most comfortable doing it), it's as if I'm watching a movie. I can see them on a blank screen in my mind's eye. That's the same screen you daydream or imagine things on. It's also the same screen where you experience memories from the past. For instance, if you close your eyes and try to recall a recent vacation you took—maybe to Disney World—you'll see the screen I am talking about. Mickey Mouse may not appear exactly as he does when you see him in person, yet you know who he is. This screen is different than your everyday field of vision—although I have seen spirits in that field of vision too, such as the ones that stood at the foot of my bed when I was little, the young girl with the burned face who appeared just after my childbearing years, or the spirits that stand behind their loved ones now when I do readings. These spirits I see in front of me instead of on my mind's screen usually have a slight tint of color to them.

That, in a nutshell, is how clairvoyance works for me, but I will tell you one more thing I find extremely interesting about this modality: The way spirits show themselves says a lot about how much free will there is on the other side. It's as much as we have here. I know this because sometimes people who died in a disfiguring accident, such as a motorcycle crash, can choose to show up in my visions looking truly awful or they can choose to look very healthy. All souls get to decide if they want to be seen in the state they were in at the moment of death or if they want to be seen in the state they were in before then. It's a lot like when you let your kid choose their school clothes for themselves. What they pick is always a statement, consciously or unconsciously. The good news is that many of them appear to me the way they looked during the best times of their lives.

Technically, *clairaudience* is when a medium experiences clear hearing. For me, a better way to describe it is to say it's a lot like listening to my own thoughts, but I'm aware that they are *not* my thoughts. It's as if these voices are coming through on a radio station. Imagine that you are traveling a long distance in your car. At some point you have to adjust the dial to get the right frequency as you are exiting one station's range and entering a new one's. When I tune in to these voices it is very much like leaving my own thoughts' radio station and picking up what's in the airwaves of the spirit world's radio station.

Clairsentience is when a medium experiences clear feelings. That can mean emotions, but more often it is actually a physical feeling. For instance, when spirits are telling me how they died, they will often make me experience the pain they felt at the time. Sometimes it's the only way they can communicate the disease or incident they suffered clearly enough. If they had a car accident, I can feel the impact they felt when they were crashing. For bus or train accidents, that impact will be even stronger. For plane accidents, I may experience the fall as well. In the case of gunshots, it will seem as if something has hit my body. I can feel myself being thrown back with force or sometimes even feel like I'm landing on concrete. But the ones that are most uncomfortable for me are the heart attacks, because they take my breath away, and lung cancer, because I will feel as if I'm choking.

I remember during one of my first readings I felt so much weight or pressure on my chest—like a huge brick—that I thought *I* was actually having a heart attack. The man I was reading for was mourning his father. They were both firemen and they were in the same house together. They were more like brothers than father and son. It was such a devastating loss for him because his dad was his best friend, his mentor, his buddy—the whole thing. This son felt so helpless because his father died right in front of him. He saw his dad clench his chest and keel over. As I was conducting this reading, I began clenching my chest too because that is how massive the pain was. I wasn't sure what was happening at first. I was very embarrassed and I kept apologizing. "I'm sorry, I'm so sorry," I said between attempts to catch my breath. And then the son validated everything: "That's exactly how my father died. He grabbed his chest and fell to the floor." At that moment it was fight or flight for me. I had to tell the father to lighten up. I spoke to him in my mind as I always speak to spirits, but I was very firm. "Please let it go. Don't make me feel your death.

Either just show it to me as a visual, like you are showing me a home movie, or tell it to me." Thankfully, my pleas worked. From that day on I made it a point to tell spirits in advance, "Tell me or show me, but please don't make me relive your pain." Most spirits don't do that, but I try to set those boundaries up front, just in case.

Another common way I will experience clairsentience is when spirits are acknowledging that a loved one is wearing or possesses an article of jewelry that connects them. The communication will usually begin with me feeling something metal between my fingers. It's the same sensation as when I hold a coin. If it is a ring they are referring to, I will also feel a heaviness on my finger. Similarly, if it's a necklace, I will feel a tugging on my neck. In either case, I will experience two sensations at once—the feeling of metal between my fingers *and* the pulling on my neck, or the feeling of metal between my fingers *and* a heaviness on my finger. This is to make sure I know we're talking about an object worn on this part of the body and not an injury the spirit sustained to this part of the body.

Sometimes the senses work together to make sure I understand the message. Let's say the item is a religious medallion. I will feel a tug on my neck followed by an image of Jesus Christ, because as a Christian this is a symbol I associate with religion. I may also see a similar pendant in my own jewelry box. So now, I am seeing *and* feeling things that help me hone in on the message. Lots of times talking to spirits can be like a game of charades— they work very hard at giving me as many clues as possible.

The next type of communication is *clairalience*, which is when a medium experiences clear smelling. I personally do not encounter this one as much as the others, but when I do, it comes as a backup or secondary source of information. The best example of this is when I am communicating with a baby spirit. He may tell me he's present by making me feel a softness between my fingers. He may follow that up by showing me his mother holding his baby blanket. For added help he may then make me smell the scent of talcum powder. Infant spirits speak to me in such creative ways—they don't have a lot of life experience so very often they will show me what is happening in their family's lives to confirm that they are still very much connected to them. Because the soul is ageless these spirits may be wise beyond their years, but they still have to act their earthly age. It can make communicating with them tough but not impossible, especially if both of us are resourceful!

There have also been times when clairalience lets me know my grandmother is around because I smell Jean Naté, the perfume she used to wear. And when my uncle Junior has a message for his family, he always sends me a whiff of his cigar smoke to let me know he's trying to communicate. When this happens, I am all ears. He has delivered several meaningful messages to his family since his passing. Most of them are of a personal nature but I can tell you that they always seem to be warnings of what is to come. My aunt and cousins appreciate the heads-up and are always amazed at the other details I relay, such as family conversations or events that happened just that week or the night before. They always follow up with the same response: "I'm sure I didn't tell you that. How do you know?" Family or not, I need to remind them that this is how I roll. LOL.

Clairgustance is when a medium experiences clear tasting. This is the least developed mode of communication for me, despite the fact that I, like everyone else, love to eat! You would think that when the best cook in a family or a celebrated chef dies and goes to heaven they might make me taste a bite of some divine dessert they were well known for as a way of communicating, but no such luck. If a chef is trying to communicate with me it is usually through visuals. Occasionally someone who loved to cook may make me taste garlic, but that's about it.

Finally, *claircognizance* is clear knowing. Quite simply, this is when you just know something even though there is no logical reason for you to know it. I'm sure you've heard people say, "I just have a gut feeling," "I have a hunch," or "I feel it in my bones." This is sometimes how mental knowing is underscored physically.

I explained all of this to you because I think it might help you understand what kind of chaos mediums often feel in their head, their body, and their life before they learn to effectively use and control their gift. If a medium has never heard or read anything about these modalities before they start occurring, it can be incredibly confusing and frightening.

Although my family had its fair share of intuitives, only my aunt in Venezuela actively practiced her gift, and the language barrier and the geographical distance between us prevented me from asking her all the questions I wanted to. It was up to me to find my own support system, and frankly, it wasn't always clear where to look and whom I could trust to give me legitimate information and insight. So keeping all these strange occurrences a secret from Holly, who I was sure would only push me to pursue my gifts before I felt comfortable enough to, wasn't easy. Yet she was the only person I could go to for clear and effective answers to my persistent questions. I mean, who else can a psychic gal approach for guidance when spirits start sending her messages in her own handwriting!

That's right, there was one more modality I was experiencing, not fully understanding, and neglecting to tell Holly about and that was automatic writing.

GETTING MY POETIC LICENSE

Around the same time that Holly was trying to convince me I had more potential than I was using, my father's brother Nunzio was tragically hit by a car. He was such a huge animal lover that he stopped on a highway to rescue a dog that had wandered into traffic. He was struck while saving this dog and died instantly. Although he lived in California and the rest of our family was located on the East Coast, he was someone who was always in our hearts and minds. He visited often and was such a big hit with all his nieces and nephews. His passing was a devastating blow to us all. My father and his siblings quickly made travel arrangements to attend the funeral. But, like me, most of my siblings and cousins had young children and couldn't get away as easily. So our generation of family decided to hold a memorial service of our own in New York. We wanted to make it a real celebration of his life. One very busy day before the service, the weirdest thing happened. I was cleaning when I looked at the clock and realized it was almost three thirty. That was the time the bus stopped in front of my house, dropping the kids off from school. It was also the time when I usually had to be ready to shuttle them to their different afternoon activities. I wasn't even dressed yet so I was really rushing. I was just about to step into the shower when a voice stopped me. It was definitely not my inner voice. I know what my own thoughts sound like and these were not them. The voice was clear and very direct. It said, "You need to write a poem for Uncle Nunzio's memorial."

I thought, "A poem? I don't write poems. What's this about?"

I started to hear the first verse when the voice stopped and commanded me to get a pen. It said, "I am going to give you the words."

To say I was resistant is a bit of an understatement. I consider myself to be a fairly logical person with practical ways of doing things, but I swear, sometimes the stuff that happens to me is just too crazy even for me to imagine!

"Not now," I thought. "I need to hop in the shower and get ready for my kids."

It was all happening in such a flash that I didn't think about *who* might have been talking to me or how disrespectful I might have sounded at that moment. There wasn't time to rationalize this whole situation. But the voice continued. I heard the poem unfolding line by line in my head. Then I felt a push, an urgency to go get that pen and some paper before I missed it all.

I was like a child refusing my parents' orders to do my homework. "Can't I do this later?" I grumbled. But the voice persisted, and then the words just started flowing. The next thing I knew, I was sitting at the kitchen table in my towel writing as fast as I could. The lines tumbled onto the page exactly the way I heard them. When it was done it was absolutely beautiful. It fit Uncle Nunzio to a tee. It read:

My Gift to All

I sent him there in '28,
To touch some lives that couldn't wait.
I called him home in '97,
To come home to live with me in heaven.
You needed him throughout the years,
Through happy times and even tears
He lent a hand to all in need
And the hungry ones he'd also feed.
He blessed you all with his brilliant smile,
Although you saw him only once in a while.
You didn't understand the life he chose,
He had his reasons that only God knows.
I gave him to all of humankind,
And another like him you will not find.
Please see he was my gift to all
But now his name I had to call.
He gave his life to save another;
He was everyone's friend and the very best brother.
He had to come from whence he came,
I held out my arms and called his name.
If he could he'd say, "Don't fear,
I'm very happy and I love it here . . .
We'll be together again once more,
I'll be here waiting at heaven's door.
You'll know it's me, I'm first in line,
You'll see my face, I'm with the divine.
I'm doing great and I'm never alone,
I just had to go back to my original home.
We never know the time or place,
But when it's time you'll see his face.
You'll try to stay with all your might,
Until you're embraced by his golden light.
You'll hear the words, 'You've done great things,
And like an angel, you've earned your wings.'

Please know from earth I had to leave,
So for my life please do not grieve.
I'll be with you always, so miss me never,
I'll see you again and it will be forever."
And the Lord said, "He set an example for all the rest,
So please understand, I take only the best!"

There are references here no one would understand unless they knew this man. So how was this voice aware of all these facts? You know, details like "He had this brilliant smile." Sure, a lot of people have nice smiles, but I swear Uncle Nunzio could have done Pepsodent commercials, his smile was so bright and welcoming. Everyone commented on it. And it's true—we all questioned the life he chose. Why did a guy who was such a family man decide to live so far away from us, especially when every time he visited it seemed like he really hated to leave. I always got the feeling that it wasn't really his choice to live way across the country. And the part about humanitarian work was spot-on too. He volunteered for so many causes. He had a heart of gold. But what kept sticking in my head was the mention of his birth date. I really had no idea what year he was born. How did the voice know it was 1928?

Well, hello, guess what? I called my cousin Mary to find out if she knew his birth date. She's the one in the family we all go to whenever we don't know something—I swear she has a computer chip in her brain. I didn't think my mother would know, and I bet if I asked my father he'd tell me they didn't even have copies of their birth certificates on the farm where they grew up in Italy. But leave it to Mary—she just happened to look up my uncle's obituary a few minutes before I called, because that's the kind of thing she does. Sure enough the date was listed as 1928. I said, "You've got to be kidding me. I just channeled a poem about him and that's the year the voice told me." No one in my family was shocked to hear about the poem at this point because wacky things were happening to me all the time now. I read it to Mary over the phone and she started crying. "Oh my God, Kim," she said. "That's going to be so comforting for the cousins to hear. It's amazing that it came to you that way." And she was right. It was amazing.

By the way, not all mediums who experience automatic writing hear dictation. Many say that they are transported while Spirit writes for them and they are only able to process what happened afterward when they read what was written.

What I take away from all these wild experiences I was having is that spirits will send you messages in whatever form they think you will hear them best. If one doesn't work, they'll try another. In my case, they hoped I would embrace at least one of these forms of communication. And when I wasn't hearing the message that mediumship was the right path for me, they repeated it until it finally got through. They spoke to me through coincidences and through every one of my senses, and when I still didn't get it, they spoke to me in poetry!

Are there recurring messages in your life you're not hearing? If so, they may very well be Spirit conducting a one-sided conversation with you. Don't wait too long to reply. Pay attention and return the call!

Chapter 8

Special Delivery

> The Joy of That First Psychic Reading

WHATEVER MAYHEM WAS OCCURRING in my life at the time, I could always count on Tuesday nights to be lots of fun. That's the evening every week that I bowled. I belonged to a league with my sister, my cousins Carm and Mary, and two really good friends, Michele and Stephanie, whom we grew up with in Ozone Park. Needless to say, when the six of us got together, the laughs kept coming. I had some of the best, best times of my life on that team.

No one ever wanted to go home when the game was over, so we'd always end up hanging out afterward. On this one night we were having a couple of drinks and laughing our asses off as usual when Michele, who was really into all of this psychic stuff, asked, "So Kim, how's it going with those psychic classes you're taking?"

"They're good, but they're all done now so I'm just reading more books on the subject."

"You doing any readings?"

I should have guessed that would be the next question. "No, I'm not at that point. It's funny you should ask, though. My mentor called me the other day to get me to do this psychic fair, but I said, 'No way.' I'm loving the past-life regression stuff much more. Maybe I'll do it at some point, but for now I have to practice."

That's when Michele took off her watch and handed it to me. "Hold it," she said. "What are you picking up?" She was another one, just like Holly, who never took no for an answer. She got right to the point. My spirit guides always knew that's how it has to be with me. To get me to do something, you have to have that kind of forward personality—unless I feel really strongly against it, and then you can't budge me. I looked at her and said, "What do you mean? What are you talking about?"

"All right, enough already. I know you can do this. What do you get from holding this watch?" she said firmly.

"Whose watch is this?" I asked.

"It's my watch."

"We did this one day in class. It's called psychometry," I explained to the others.

So I held Michele's watch and, after tuning in for a second or two, I said to her, "I'm hearing this guy. Somebody's coming through, but I can't make out what he's saying."

"Go on, go on. Keep talking."

"He's saying something about his lever. I don't know what this is, but he keeps saying 'My lever, my lever.'"

"Oh my God, I know what you're getting."

"Michele, I can't go any further. What does this mean, 'a lever'?" I kept thinking it was a tool of some kind.

She said, "It's my father-in-law. He died of liver disease and he has a thick Italian accent. That's how he says *liver*."

I was stunned. "Oh my God. Really? You think so?"

"Kim, he just died last week."

"Michele, I'm so sorry. I didn't even know."

"He was sick for a while. It was a terrible loss but also a relief to know he was finally out of his pain. Keep going, keep going," she encouraged me. She obviously wanted to hear more from him.

"All right. He's saying something about Anna."

"That's my mother-in-law. That's his wife."

It all started coming to me after that. I was seeing pictures in my head. As I started relaying the images to her I said, "Michele, I'm just telling you the pictures I'm seeing and what I hear."

"Kim, that's great. You're nailing it, you're nailing it. Everything you're seeing is right."

"Wait, he's saying something about someone named Gertrude and how she didn't come to the wake because they're not talking."

At that point Michele was beside herself. "You're *freaking* me out. Gertrude *didn't* come to the wake. My God!"

All I could think was "What's going on? This is crazy!" At that moment something switched and I started hearing the name Larry. I asked Michele who he was but she didn't seem to know.

"Well, that's what I'm hearing," I told her. "I'm hearing the name Larry. Someone's screaming in my ear, 'Just say Larry, Larry.'"

At that point Stephanie's phone rang. It was late—twelve thirty or a quarter to one in the morning. She looked at the caller ID and said that it was her good friend—a woman who had a young son with some health issues. We all immediately started worrying that the call was related to him. Stephanie quickly answered and as she listened to the voice on the other end, her eyes grew wide. Now we're all sitting with baited breath. We wanted to know what happened.

"What?! Larry got shot?! Oh my God, is he okay?" she asked.

I was dumbfounded at this point. Not more than two seconds earlier I was saying that I was hearing the name Larry. Then the phone rang with the news that a Larry one of us knew was just shot.

"Who died? What's going on?" we were all asking at once. When she hung up the phone she told us that her husband's best friend, Larry, just got shot.

"Is he dead? Because I think I'm channeling him," I piped in.

"I don't know, I don't know. He's being rushed to the hospital right now."

We all looked at each other in disbelief.

Michele broke the silence. "You know you're picking this stuff up, right? You're a medium and you don't even know it. You have no idea what you're sitting on."

As it turned out Larry miraculously lived, but I wouldn't find that out until a few days later. I think I was just tuning in to his frequency as events were unfolding.

I still couldn't make sense of what happened by the time I got home. I was thinking it was all a fluke. I couldn't trust that I'd ever be able to give an accurate reading again. I honestly believed that I just got lucky.

The next morning at ten o'clock my phone rang. It was Michele.

"Do you know my head is still spinning from last night?" she said excitedly. "I told my husband all about his father coming through. I called my brother too. In fact, I called my whole family."

I knew her parents and all of her brothers from the old neighborhood.

"Kim, you have to do me a favor. You've got to tell my brother something. His best friend died recently and he desperately needs to hear something from him. I told him about last night and I know you can help him."

I panicked. "Michele, don't do this to me," I said. "I don't know if I can help him. I think last night was a fluke. I don't have any objects of his. Next time I see him I'll try to hold his watch or something. Maybe I can pick something up for him then."

She wasn't backing down. "Kim, you've got to do this for him. He's here now. He came over just to talk to you."

"All right, put him on the phone," I relented. "But I can't promise you anything."

When her brother got on the line I could already hear gratitude and anticipation in his voice. "Hey, Kim. How are you?"

"Listen, I'm really sorry about your friend. I'd love to help you, but I don't know if I'm a medium. The best I can do is what I did with your sister last night. If pictures come flooding into my mind or if I hear anything, I'm just going to tell you what I see and hear."

"All right. It's no big deal. If that's all you can do, don't worry, but I really miss him. He was my buddy, you know? I'd just love to hear from him."

I took a deep breath and began letting the messages come to me. I got his name right off the bat. "It's something with a G—Gary or Greg." Then I said, "He's showing me a car," and I began describing it to him.

"Go ahead, go ahead. I understand that."

"He's got the hood of the car up. You know what it looks like to me? Was he a mechanic?"

"Why are you asking that?"

"Because he's showing me this car in the middle of the Friendly Frost parking lot. I don't know if his car used to break down all the time and he had to fix it a lot or what. But he has the hood of the car lifted up and his head is under it, poking around at the engine."

He started hysterically laughing and just said, "I understand what that means."

Now here I am still in the dark. I want to understand what that means too. "I don't want to keep going until I know that I'm getting it right," I told him.

"Well, it's a little embarrassing."

"Embarrassing or not, I need to know."

"He used to steal cars from that lot and that's how he'd get them started. He told me about it years later." He paused and added, "Can you just ask him if he's okay?"

When I confirmed that he was doing just fine, Michele's brother seemed so happy to hear it. I suspect it gave him some closure to know a friend he worried about was okay on the other side.

After the reading was over, I sat there and thought, "This is just bonkers. I'm channeling spirits during past-life regressions with Anthony, taking dictation from them after the passing of loved ones, seeing apparitions, hearing spirits' voices in my head day and night, and now seeing clear enough images on the screen in my mind to conduct spontaneous readings!" The pace of these incidents picked up so rapidly that I wasn't sure how to stop it all. The only person I knew who could advise me was Holly. The psychic fair was just one week away and I was sure if I asked her for help she was going to pressure me into reading with her at the event. But it got so nuts that I had to put an end to it. I finally gave in and called Holly.

"Holly, it's Kim," I said. "I really need your help."

"What's the matter?"

"Well, you were right. It's true. Spirit has been trying to tell me something and I haven't wanted to listen."

"Why don't you fill me in on what's been happening?"

After I gave her all the details about the girl who died in the fire, Uncle Nunzio, the night we all went bowling, and the reading the next morning, she very predictably said, "I told you, Kim." I can still hear her gentle laugh in my ear. "Now will you do the fair?" she asked.

When I said no, she guilted me in the way every loving Jewish or Italian mother does when she knows what's best for her kids. She said, "Listen to me very carefully, sweetheart. This has nothing to do with you. Spirit wants to use your voice. That's all this is, honey. I promise you, I'll be right there to help you. If you get stuck, I'll swoop in and take over. But I know from experience that once you do a reading you will learn to trust Spirit. Now you're telling me you did two readings—and they were fabulous. Can't you see? The door has already been opened, Kim. Spirits are knocking. If you say no now, they're going to move on and they're never coming back. You're going to lose the opportunity of a lifetime. This is the very reason why you were born."

"What, to be a medium?" I was really pushing back now. "I don't know that I want that responsibility. It's a lot of pressure to always have to deliver the goods. What if I get it wrong? What if one time I'm really off base? I don't want to deliver a message that's not clear or that can be misinterpreted in any way. I spent my whole lifetime being logical about everything I ever did. It seems to me that being a medium is too much like being a doctor. I'd always have to be on call and people would always be looking to me for answers. It is already happening to me. This is not what I want."

"But sometimes it's not about what you want, Kim. You picked this before you were born. Although you're just remembering that agreement now, it was made a long time ago. I assure you, once you embrace this truth, life's going to be so much easier for you. You have to do the fair, Kim. I'm sorry. I'll teach you to control how and when the voices speak to you, but just know they won't stop until you agree to *be* their voice."

And that's when it hit me. I thought about all the times I was sure I knew what was good for me only to find out later that I was completely wrong. Memories from my dating years came flooding back to me. I recalled how twice I persisted in stubbornly thinking I knew love, but when I surrendered myself to the Universe I was led to the person who showed me the kind of love that was best for me.

I remembered regretfully the girl who died in the fire—the one with the burned face—and how she was relying on me to get a message through to her parents, and I didn't do it. I knew now that I shouldn't be resisting Holly's advice. I had to surrender to what she was telling me. All the people being put on my path were reminding me of what I signed on for. I never ever claimed to know everything—maybe this was as good a time as any to learn new things. All signs were pointing in that direction.

I was beginning to realize that I was a beacon of light. That somehow the Universe was shining that light through me, drawing guiding forces *and* spirits in need of my help to me. Yes, it was a huge responsibility to be a voice for the other side, but who can say no to a mission ordained by the Divine?

Finally, I gave in and committed to doing the fair.

SETTING THE GROUND RULES

I was so nervous that whole week. I worried about what would happen if Spirit didn't come to me during each of the readings. I had no backup plan. I wouldn't lie to people—I *couldn't* lie to them! But just as Holly promised, Spirit did come to me, and we managed to pull it all off together without a hitch. People were lining up to see me. And all Holly kept doing was smiling and winking in my direction. As folks left satisfied with what they heard, the line grew. She saw the line, and I saw it too. I couldn't catch my breath between readings, because despite proof that connections were being made, I kept wondering if Spirit would tire or my luck would run out. But Spirit stuck with me through to the very last reading of the day.

Just to make sure I didn't miss the point, the following week Spirit revealed itself to me in yet another tremendous way. Holly always recognized a connection to Spirit when she saw it and was quick to request a conversation. Once she finally witnessed the abilities she was so sure

I had, she wanted me to give her a personal reading. She was having a very difficult time in her life, and she was hoping the other side could provide some insight. I couldn't say no, so we met at a local diner. We planned to do the reading and then enjoy lunch together. As you know by now, Holly taught us how to open our channels up before a reading and how to close them down when we were through. I must have been distracted by our conversation or the meal that followed—or maybe I just wasn't practiced enough—but I forgot to close myself off this time. In the booth next to us, there was an elderly woman, her husband, and a younger man. I whispered to Holly, "Do you see those people to my left? One of their dead relatives is coming through to me. Somebody keeps saying, 'Leslie, Leslie, Leslie.'" (In those days, the spirit would repeat its name until I would say it aloud.) Holly sprang into action: "Honey, you know you have to deliver the message."

"No, I am *not* doing that," I said. "I'm telling you so you can give them the message. You're my teacher. I don't want to do it. I want to see you read."

She laughed. "Kim, they're not coming to me, they're coming to you. I'm not hearing their words, you are."

Then do you know what she did? She turned around to get their attention. "Excuse me, I don't mean to bother you, but my friend and I are both psychics and she's a medium. I believe my friend has a message for you. One of your loved ones is trying to contact you through her."

At this point I was dying. I couldn't believe what she was doing. She gave me no choice. I finally said, "I'm so sorry. I don't normally interrupt strangers' meals, but there's a persistent spirit who is letting me know he has a message for you. I feel compelled to deliver it. Do you know anyone named Leslie?"

The woman's face dropped. She looked at her husband and then said, "I certainly do."

"Well, someone from the spirit world keeps telling me, 'Please say my name is Leslie.'"

"That's my son. I lost my son," the woman said.

I was a little surprised. "Your son's name is *Leslie*?" That's a pretty uncommon name for a male.

"No, no. I was married before, so that's his last name."

"Well, he just wants you to know that he's okay." I just wanted to end the awkwardness and get back to my salad but I heard something more from him, so I relayed that too. "Oh, and he's saying the name Sandra as well."

"Oh my God! That's my daughter. That's his sister."

"I don't know what more to tell you. That's what he communicated to me."

"I'm speechless. I don't know who you are."

I could see then that she was visibly shaken by the experience. "Please, I hope I didn't hurt or offend you in any way, but the spirit was so strong and I'm a medium, I just had to tell you. He wouldn't let up until I said something." I felt awful. She was bawling her eyes out as the three of them got up at once to leave the restaurant. She didn't even finish her meal.

Her husband kept saying, "Honey, come on. We've got to go."

It was nuts. I couldn't believe what was happening. I really didn't know if her husband was upset with me or frightened. He just rushed his wife out of there. But then the young man who was with them came back and asked if he could have my telephone number. I gave it to him, but I was doubtful I'd ever hear from them again. I traumatized that poor woman.

Holly felt differently, of course. She firmly believed that you have to honor Spirit when Spirit comes, no matter what. "Those are the rules. Do you know how much energy it takes for that spirit to show himself? If he made the effort, you must too. *You always have to deliver the message*," she said forcefully.

Neither she nor Spirit ever had to tell me that again. I knew she was right, so I set up a private space in my home to make spirit communication through me more practical. Michele told her friends, and everybody started calling me.

I decided I was not going to charge anybody for at least one year, while I was still learning Spirit's language. If people wanted to leave me a tip, they could do so *after* the reading, but as a "medium intern," which is how I thought of myself, I just didn't feel comfortable accepting fees.

Would you believe that Sandra was among my first clients that year? She tried every trick in the book to withhold her identity from me—including fibbing about some things—because she was skeptical about my abilities and was trying to test me after hearing about what happened to her mother in the diner. Spirit wasn't having any of that, though. Her brother came through to me quickly and revealed who she was. We talked more, and what I relayed confirmed that I was legit. She came to see me many more times after that, as did her mother. I was sad to hear a year or so down the road that Sandra's mother passed, but I took comfort in the fact that she had been reunited with her son.

In retrospect I think it was important that they were in the first wave of people who came to see me. It proved to them and to me that mediumship is really possible. People cannot be fooled. They especially cannot be fooled day in and day out, year after year, reading after reading. The experiences we had—the spirit energy we felt—were very tangible. If mediumship was not for real I would never have been able to share such accurate information with them and I certainly would never have been able to survive my first year, let alone the nearly two decades that followed. The constant stream of referrals coming to me for the same quality experience their friends have had before them is further proof.

I learned so much from Holly, my visits to the library, and my amazing spirit guides during that fruitful period that I thought it might be helpful to include some of my early lessons for you here.

READINGS 101

The first order of business was to set up signals with Spirit to indicate when I was ready to receive messages. Holly told me that I needed to start a dialogue with my spirit guides right away and that they would help train me since they knew all the workings on the other side. When I told Holly I didn't know any spirit guides, she was adamant that it didn't matter. (Remember, although I introduced Kali to you earlier because of her wisdom on relationships, I hadn't met her until Holly's class introduced me to past-life regressions and I began trying them on my own.) "They're present for you already," she assured me. "You just need to recognize that they're there. The minute you believe they are with you and you trust that they will *always* be with you, your life as a medium is going to get a lot easier."

"Okay, so what do I tell them once I acknowledge their presence?"

"Tell them you need to set a boundary and that an on-duty sign would help. Then pick whatever sign you want to send them and let them know what that sign will be." When I wasn't sure what she meant, she suggested that maybe I ring a bell to say, "Okay, I'm ready for you to come forward now."

What crystallized this whole signaling process for me, though, was when she gave me the example of how children will persist when they want your attention. "If you are in the middle of something, you either tell them to wait or you ignore them until you're ready to listen. It's the same way with dead people. You need to tell them you're not ready yet. You have to be direct. Let them know you need your space, you have a family, and you will listen to them when you're good and ready—when you can give them your undivided attention, and not a moment before then." With three young boys at home, I understood this logic perfectly.

Then, of course, I had to establish a signal to tell spirits when I was done for the day. Holly's recommendations made me laugh. "Some mediums go to bed with a hat on," she said. "And once that hat goes on it's like they're saying they're closing up shop for the night." She also told me that some mediums sleep with a towel over their head so their Crown chakra remains closed.

Since you'd never catch me going to bed with a hat on—it just isn't my style—I decided I would light a candle whenever I wanted to signal I was open for messages. I figured that when spirits saw the flame of my candle they would know that it was okay to stop by, because lighting a candle, after all, represents connecting to the light. When I was done I would simply blow the candle out. I thought that was a really clever solution. But there was one problem: I was a total candle burner even before I came up with the idea of applying it as my symbol. I used to light them all the time because I loved the way they made my house smell. I especially relied on their scent when I was cooking fish. But to prevent my house from filling up with spirits 24/7 and defeating the purpose of the signal altogether, I decided to keep the candle as my symbol with spirits and I switched to using essential oils and a diffuser every time I wanted to enjoy fresh aromas in my home. It worked, and everyone was happy.

"Deliver the mail; don't read it" is an important rule I had to learn *right away.* (Note: This shouldn't be confused with the "you *must* deliver the message" rule noted earlier, as they are two distinct concepts.) As I met with more clients, I realized that spirits choose to appear to me in the way they believe they'll be most recognizable to the people they are speaking to. A perfect example of this is when a fifty-year-old man who lost his mother when he was only ten came for a reading, his mother purposely appeared as she did just before she died. Although it took a minute for me to register that this young-looking woman was this older man's mother, it took the son only a nanosecond to recognize her description, because that is exactly how he remembered her.

A way more specific example of needing to be attentive to this rule came up for me in a house reading. An entire family was present when I brought a woman's father through. Everyone in the family was hoping to hear from him. After he told me his name and how he died, he shared a number of other details that resonated with everyone there, but they all seemed to be waiting for me say one thing in particular. I had seen it right off the bat and recognized it as a hint of some kind. The man was wearing a red-checkered flannel shirt, and I knew I was supposed to bring that up because I had never seen a spirit wearing one of those before. It really seemed out of the ordinary. Most spirits show themselves to me from the neck up, so when I see them in a particular outfit I know there's more to the story. When I mentioned that shirt to the family, there was instant validation. Apparently the man owned twenty of them. He didn't wear the same exact shirt every day, but red-checkered flannel shirts were the only type he ever wore. They didn't know why. They just knew he loved them. He wore that style shirt in the winter, spring, summer, and fall. It soon became a trademark of his. They were hoping and praying that this detail would come through. This spirit knew that was the only thing I needed to say for his loved ones to believe my reading, so he came properly attired. But had I tried to interpret that sign in any way, I would have blown it. For instance, if I had asked, "Is your father a farmer?" because I associate red-checkered flannel shirts with this type of work, they would have thought I was way off base. Anything I'd said before then that rang true to them would be called into question. My own frame of reference would have clearly mucked things up. I learned very early on not to try to figure out why a spirit is showing himself in a certain way. Now I just let people know what I see. That's what I mean when I say just "deliver the mail." The mailman doesn't know what the letter he is bringing to your doorstep is about or what it means; he just knows he needs to deliver it the way it's intended to be delivered—unopened and unread.

One time before I fully understood this rule, there was a very strong spirit who shouted out of sheer frustration, "Just say what you see!" That's right, a spirit yelled at me. He wasn't my guide—he was a spirit. He got very stern with me because, as Holly mentioned earlier, it takes a lot for souls on the other side to be able to communicate with us. When the person he was speaking to through me couldn't understand my take on what he was trying to convey, he had had enough and told me so. From that point on I never made that mistake again. In the case of the house reading, if I asked the family "Is your dad a farmer?" I would have been wrong. Instead the better question to ask is "Does a red-checkered flannel shirt mean anything to you?" Bingo. This kind of unfiltered approach seems to work every time. Through that kind of trial and error I learned the language of Spirit.

Spirit Shorthand

Speaking of language, Spirit and I developed a kind of shorthand to help us communicate faster, and it was, in fact, based on visual symbols. But for the most part these symbols were taught to me in advance so no interpretation would be required after the first few times I encountered them. Let me explain what I mean.

I realized early on that spirits can't always sustain their energy for a long time. When they come to me they need to lower their vibrations and I need to raise mine. Adjusting ourselves this way is a lot like asking us to hop on one foot for twenty minutes—it's going to take a ton of energy. My guides heard these concerns, and their response in those early months was very clever. For one straight week they would send me only people who had passed by suicide. It was nonstop. Every reading was with a soul who had taken their own life. Then the next week every spirit who spoke to me was killed in a car accident. The following week everyone who came through died because of a drug overdose. My guides set these readings up this way purposely to help me learn the symbols for each fatal event. It was no coincidence that they were sending me the same type of people with the same types of deaths. This was their lesson plan. This was how they taught me that when you see this particular recurring image it means it was cancer, or it was diabetes, and so on. It was really an ingenious way to tutor me!

The following are examples of some symbols that were repeatedly shown to me and have become part of my spiritual dialogue used to this day. Many are obvious, because Spirit is interested in being as clear as possible so the delivered message is accurate. Others are symbols that grew out of my own associations. Of course Spirit can't possibly anticipate a symbol for every situation I encounter, so I must simply relay what I see in those instances. You never know—a new symbol may emerge out of the experience.

ILLNESSES

Brain trauma or a brain tumor is indicated by the person pointing to his head.

A stroke is indicated by a large red clot wedged in a vessel.

Heart and vascular diseases, including conditions leading to them such as high blood pressure, high cholesterol, and diabetes, are indicated by a large red clot located near the heart.

Blood diseases such as HIV or AIDS are often indicated by a battle between white blood cells and red blood cells.

Cancer is indicated by dark spots in the area where the cancer is concentrated. When it rises from a lower area to a higher area it indicates that it is metastasizing.

Cancers of the blood, including leukemia, myeloma, or lymphoma, are often indicated by a nurse standing over a patient with vials of blood. This can also indicate the need for blood transfusions.

Lung cancer is indicated by an image of dark spots on the lungs or by my having difficulty breathing. Although I've asked spirits not to make me feel uncomfortable, they may share their illnesses with me in this way because it may be in their nature—in life as well as in the afterlife—to provide all the gory details when relaying their story. Spirits aren't always fluent in the language of psychic mediumship either. If this is their first attempt at communicating through a medium, it may take them several tries before they get the hang of doing it just right.

Breast cancer is indicated by a pea-size lump inside the breasts. If it's fatal, I will often get a sinking feeling in my stomach. Remission is accompanied by a level feeling, and in some instances a feeling of hope.

Arthritis is often spelled out for me or is indicated by the image of twisted fingers.

Fibromyalgia is indicated by my muscles aching for a split second.

Muscular, joint, or back injury is indicated by pain in my corresponding body part.

Tendons in need of repair or knees in need of replacement are indicated by pain in these corresponding areas on my body or my seeing kneecaps in my third eye. (This chakra will be addressed further in chapter 9.)

OCCUPATIONS

A nurse or a teacher is indicated by an image of helping hands.

A police officer, firefighter, or military personnel is indicated by an image of helping hands in conjunction with a big building or with a blue uniform (even people in the army are depicted in blue uniforms for me).

A mechanic, electrician, or IT specialist is indicated by an image of wires. I will actually see the Verizon logo if he works for a phone company; the LIPA (Long Island Power Authority) or Con Edison logos if he works for a utility company; and the Apple logo if he works with computers.

An accountant or financial planner is indicated by numbers over one's head.

Someone in food preparation or the hospitality industry is indicated by images of a bar, restaurant, baked goods, or meats.

A healer is indicated by light (sometimes rainbow-colored) coming from one's hands. A funnel-shaped light at the top of one's head also indicates healing or psychic abilities, or that she channels spirits.

A lawyer is indicated by an image of contracts being signed or the facade of a law firm. Someone consulting a lawyer or going through the process of divorce may also be indicated by these same images.

A musician or someone who has musical abilities is indicated by musical notes.

A band member is indicated by the image of a guitar or drum set.

An architect or engineer or someone remodeling their home is indicated by an image of floor plans.

RANDOM IMAGES

An X over an object means something shouldn't be done, or it has stopped.

A book indicates that someone is writing one or she is reading one at the moment that resonates with what she is interested in.

A dog or cat indicates that a pet sees spirits or is in the spirit world.

A green light means the spirit agrees with what this person is doing and is encouraging them to move forward.

Steps or a staircase means the person is getting a raise or is going to the next level in her life. For instance, she may be getting married, buying a house, or expecting a baby.

Specific numbers indicate a special date to be remembered, for example, the age at which a person died, the month or date that she passed, the anniversary of her death, or a birthday.

Birds, butterflies, pennies, dimes, a car radio, or a digital clock indicate that a spirit is around you and sending you signs.

A glass of brandy or scotch in one's hand indicates that he is more than an occasional drinker.

Boxes indicate a recent or upcoming move to a new home or job.

A cell-phone invoice indicates that a person will get caught cheating or is being followed by someone.

Dating websites such as Match.com indicate a person will meet someone new online or through a social network.

A *barbecue or summer event* indicates a family reunion or an encounter that can develop into a relationship.

A *turkey for Thanksgiving, a Christmas tree for the winter holidays, fireworks for the Fourth of July,* or some symbol closely tied to a holiday indicates an event, passing, or birthday that occurred around that time.

Parallel lines indicate that two events happened close together or that there is a similarity between two people being discussed.

A *heart shape on a sleeve* indicates that a person wears his heart on his sleeve and is too easygoing or needs to set boundaries in his life.

A *doormat* indicates the person has insecurities.

A *rainbow in the sky* indicates there will be a good outcome regardless of how things seem.

The ocean indicates an upcoming or recent trip, or a cruise across the water.

A *map of the United States or the shape of a state* indicates a person has some connection to that place or will be traveling there soon.

Ovaries or a uterus indicate the person is going through in vitro fertilization, is having a hard time conceiving, or could not have children.

One of the other important rules I learned in a hurry during that first year was that mediums work for both sides—the living and the departed. There was a time when I was doing a reading for a woman whose dead father came through. She told me in no uncertain terms that she didn't want to talk to him. Now I was in a tight spot. I said, "Well, he wants to talk to you. He says he wants to apologize to you for the many, many things he did." He wasn't talking generalities. He listed several very specific acts. I could tell by the woman's body language that what I was relaying was totally on target. At that point she said to me, "I have spent my whole life making his life easy. I made him look good to other people. I made excuses for him, and I am telling you I am not going to placate or comfort him now, even in his death, because he made my life that miserable." She was so fired up that she continued: "I took the fall for him. I covered for him. And he didn't do anything for me." I felt for her. I really did. I will never forget this reading. But at the same time I had to tell her, "You need to understand that I don't just work for you—I work for him too. I'm a mediator. I'm not judging you and I'm not judging him. I'm here to relay his message. Presumably he just heard what you said in response. You need to work this out or he wouldn't be showing up right now. His soul can't move forward without your forgiveness." And that's when she said, "I'm not ready to forgive him, so if he can't move on, too bad for him." Of course, I couldn't make her do anything she didn't want to do, but I had to represent both sides. Maybe I didn't help resolve the situation right then and there, but I like to think that the reading helped to broaden her view of what happens on the other side—of what her father was now dealing with.

When we leave this earth we don't just bask in the sun all day. Far from it. We see things from an aerial view. Our perspective is no longer limited by factors such as our upbringing, our fears, or our insecurities. When you get to the other side there are a lot of things you don't take with you, such as clinical depression or addiction. So when you experience the flashback of your life, you see it with the clear eyes of the soul. It's a complete view. You see all the things you couldn't see when you were living—the things that may have been blocked from your vision for whatever reasons. The soul has to wrestle with that view, and communicating apologies for past hurts is one aspect of what I do to help those souls. That's the part of me that is working for both sides.

Most Frequently Asked Questions

By the way, I discovered even before the reading for the woman who didn't want to speak to her father that people come to mediums with a checklist of expectations. If even one of these requirements isn't met, they will sometimes question the validity of what they've heard.

THE CHECKLIST

¤ Most people want me to speak about the loved one they came to hear from, even if someone else they know comes through with an important or powerful message.

¤ They want me to know their loved one's name. Even the most intimate details no one else could possibly know will mean nothing to them without the name to back it up.

¤ Of course, they want to know if their loved ones made it safely to the other side and are happy.

¤ They also want to know who else is there with their loved one. They want to be assured that this soul is not alone.

¤   Very often, I will be asked if their loved one can come to visit them again and if so, how they can encourage them to do this. I must always tell them that this is not a good idea. Asking your dead relative to appear to you in full-body apparition after they have entered the light is like asking them to hike down a steep mountain they just climbed up. It is way too taxing for them. The only time you may see them is immediately after they have died. They may come around to the foot of your bed to say good-bye before they ascend to the light. But be assured that after that they are still around you in a less visible way and can send signs that let you know this is so.

¤   Another popular question is "Does my loved one miss me?" Of course, I have to explain that missing someone requires the passing of time, but without the concept of time on the other side there is no longing in the way we know it here. That is a good thing. Sure, your loved ones in spirit miss your kisses and maybe they even miss your meatballs, but they can be with you every day, especially for Sunday dinners when their favorite foods are on the menu. Though you should remember that they have no need for physical pleasures without a body. They are there to savor memories, not the meal, and are content just to be in your company.

¤   Invariably people will also want to know if they did everything to their loved one's liking before that special someone died.

¤   After hitting all of these key points they will want their loved one to talk about what they see for them. It's human nature. They might ask, "Does my mother have any insight into my current health?" "Should I marry the man I'm dating?" "Is this pending job offer right for me?"

Many people are under the misconception that when their relatives pass on, they are suddenly privy to all of the mysteries of the Universe and can now provide answers to the many burning questions we have too. Even though these departed souls have a much broader perspective once they get to the other side, a more complete picture is only revealed to them over time. And what additional insight they do have does not always come with the right to interfere with the law of free will. Please remember too that your deceased loved one's personality stays intact once they gain entrance through the pearly gates. If you had a mom who was always interfering and sticking her nose where it doesn't belong, then most likely the Akashic information about your life will be concealed from her until she understands the proper protocol and use of this information. What these souls can offer us instead of absolute answers is their opinion or advice, just as they would offer us it if they were still alive. Because we are still on our journey toward Enlightenment even after we cross over, it is important to remember that your mother's advice is probably coming from only a slightly more expanded mind-set than she had while she was still alive.

After thousands of readings, I have learned that it is best not to pray to your deceased loved ones for answers or for the desires of your heart, as they only have so much power and need to appeal to a higher level of authority to even get involved. Besides, as many deceased loved ones tell me, the answers aren't always guaranteed, as the outcome depends as much upon the choices their living relative makes through their own free will. But take heart, as there are exceptions. Your deceased loved ones may get permission to intervene in order to keep you safe and out of danger. They do this by sending you warning signs to change the unfavorable results of a circumstance. There are many crafty ways in which a spirit can send you such signs. Sometimes they can appear in a dream. They can come directly through a medium, or they can arrive via messages from one of your very good friends. Remember the car radio with Anthony and his grandfather? You just need to be open to recognizing the signs once they are sent. And remember what I told you about your various spirit guides and angels? They are typically the ones who step forward during a reading to steer you when it comes to your life path and major decision-making. They are commissioned by God to help you make the best choices in order to stay on your soul's path, achieving the best results for all concerned.

Of course, the person's spirit guide can't interfere either, but during a reading they often step forward to offer information that can help the person navigate their life better. That's when I go into full psychic journalist mode and start asking the spirit guide what this person has to learn. Why, when, and with whom? I can dig into the Akashic records too. Then I can reveal things to the person I am reading for that *remind* them of their mission so they can decide for themselves if this path is best for their health, if this person is the one to marry, or if that job is the one to take. This is where my unending curiosity really comes in handy. For instance, if someone is involved in a relationship with an abusive partner, and the details of this abuse come through from the other side, the person will feel discomfort or shame knowing that their mother is able to witness this truth too. "They can see that?" they always ask. Somehow this reflection of their own life through the eyes of a loved one who has passed is enough for the person to decide for themselves what they will do about their situation. No advice needs to be given.

By the end of that first year, I knew that this gift I had was a huge responsibility. But now that I really was an active medium, I was feeling good about my work, even on days when I hit snags. Holly was teaching me. Spirit was teaching me. And so were the people I was reading for.

Before I close this chapter, I must mention that my dear friend and mentor Holly Chalnick passed away in March 2010, leaving a huge hole in my heart. She visited me one day shortly afterward to assure me that she is happy and well on the other side. It was a cold day and I remember carefully navigating the ice on the ground after a bad storm. My focus was completely on keeping my footing so I wouldn't fall, when all of a sudden I heard her call my name. Her face was right there in front of mine. It was just like her to try to get my attention when I was focused on something completely different. Although Holly had many gifts, her best was as a teacher. I can't say which served me better, her wisdom or her persistence, but I'm grateful for both. I have felt her presence with me several times while writing this book, and I know she is genuinely happy so many of her psychic predictions for me have come true. I am glad you got to meet her too, in a way.

Chapter 9

Don't All Talk at Once

AFTER REALIZING HOW MUCH these messages were helping people heal, I knew I couldn't turn back. There was no way I could let these folks down. And the people surrounding me knew it too. Every waking moment between cooking dinner, doing homework with my kids, and listening to my husband recount the events of his day was spent on the phone or meeting with grieving people, connecting them with their loved ones. They were hanging on my every word so I had to give them my full attention. Somehow speaking with me sustained their sanity. Of course, I felt I had to comply. But as their needs became more and more demanding it was apparent that I had to rethink how I was approaching this whole process. I never wanted to lose the passion that was burning inside of me to do this work, but I knew if I didn't set some boundaries and revise the ground rules soon, I would resent my decision to share my gift with the world. Our family was growing and so were its needs. Unfortunately there were many days when I spent more time talking to the dead than the living. Even late at night the phone would ring. "Can I ask you just one question?" And of course, their heart-wrenching pleas would convince me to oblige.

The call that changed everything, though, came during dinner one evening. I was enjoying a nice conversation with my husband and children when the phone rang. I picked it up as always and ended up missing the rest of the meal as a result. The woman on the line wanted me to give her a sample reading before she would book an appointment with me. Can you believe that? She told me that all her friends said I was great but she wasn't sure she wanted to waste time coming to see me if I wasn't the real thing. She flat out asked, "Could you just tell me something about myself before I book?" I was usually very diplomatic and respectful, but this time I had to say exactly what I was thinking without censoring myself. "To be honest with you, I can't. That's not how I work," I said. "When you go for a haircut you don't ask the stylist for a sample and then say, 'Okay, you can finish the rest of the cut now,' do you?" That's exactly the image that came to my mind. I visualized her walking into a salon and asking them to cut just one side so she could decide if she wanted them to do the other one too. After some back and forth, I finally said, "I respect your position but I cannot honor your request. You know what, why don't you think about it and get back to me when you're ready?" She said, "No, no, no. I want to book an appointment now."

At that moment, I realized that while I didn't necessarily want to charge for my healing gift, I should definitely be charging for my time away from my family.

When I returned to the table, my husband, who overheard the whole crazy exchange, asked me a few questions: "Honey, do you still worry that these abilities of yours are not real? That you're going to sit down for a reading one day and nothing is going to come to you?" I got his point but he continued. "Has that ever happened to you during this entire year you've been doing these readings? Has there ever been a time when a spirit was a no-show? Or when you disappointed a client?" I didn't even have to think about the answer. It was easy. "No. Never. Some readings were better than others, and I learned why with each one. But no, I never had that happen."

At that point Anthony offered a solution. "People need spiritual insights and messages and you need a job with a salary," he said. "I think we can find a happy medium. Why don't you start charging a reasonable fee for what you're doing? I'll help by answering the phones."

I finally agreed. My very supportive husband understood that I had a mission to fulfill and he was even willing to join forces with me to help accomplish it. He began keeping my calendar, fielding all the calls, and setting up my appointments. My problem was solved. He immediately instituted a very efficient scheduling system—all those with "just one question" were put on a waiting list, while those with more pressing needs were given priority. There were so many requests that the wait was soon three years long!

Occasionally someone would cancel, allowing us to move on to the next name on the list earlier than expected. Many times when people got through due to a cancellation, their loved ones in Spirit would tell me that they were responsible for getting them the appointment. I quickly began to see a pattern. The spirit world was actively involved in manipulating my calendar! Don't ask me how they did it, but they inspired Anthony to offer available appointments to the right client on such important dates as the anniversary of their death, their wedding, their birthday, or other momentous occasions. The domino effect was in play—Anthony was helping me, and the spirit world was helping both of us to help others.

NEW RULES

I knew these weren't the only changes that needed to happen. If I was to help more people, I would have to conduct my readings more effectively too. *I began to teach Spirit how to teach me.* I went down the FAQ checklist. I wanted to know how I could get a spirit to give me his name without having to pry it out of him. So I thought, "What if my guides asked everyone who came forward to whisper their name in my ear? Would that work?" Together we figured out that it would work, but that it might also be good if they spelled their names out visually, as if on a chalk or Smart Board. This way I could read them and there would be no confusion when it came to uncommon names. Bingo! Problem solved. (Remember, at this point in my practice of mediumship I was talking to only the more cooperative spirits who had crossed over into the light. I hadn't yet discovered how to effectively talk with the trapped spirits who were still struggling to find their way between the earthly and heavenly planes.)

Of course there are always spirits who like to have a little fun with me. Some have even used pictograms to help me out. Once during a reading, I asked a woman, "Is there a reason why I'm seeing a big red juicy steak over your head?" Her response was "My family name is Salisbury." We got a good laugh at her loved one's ingenuity. Writing it out wouldn't have been nearly as humorous as showing it to me. Another time I saw a baby-grand piano above someone's head only to find out that her family name was Piano. I'd never heard of such a name and there would have been no other way for me to figure it out. She even offered to show me her license as proof, but I trusted Spirit.

Next was the question, "Who else is my departed loved one with?" Answering that was always tricky because then the person would want to hear from all the others too. This required a more complete understanding of how the different levels work on the other side of the veil. So I observed, and later it was confirmed for me, that the spirits occupying the higher levels are free to travel to the lower levels whenever they want, while those on the lower levels are restricted from roaming anywhere else above them. Given this little clearance issue, I had to find a place where every spirit who wanted to be present for the reading could gather easily. So going forward, I always set the meeting space on the entry level where the souls first arrive after physical death—the level commonly referred to as the astral plane. This level of existence can be looked at as a transitional space or as a doorway to access the higher planes. This panned out well for everyone. Because mediums must raise their vibrations to speak to spirits, and spirits must lower their vibrations to speak to mediums, gathering at a lower level that is not too high up makes it accessible to all who have transitioned into the light, and prevents us all from having to strain too much to communicate. The quality of the readings dramatically improved!

Now I was really onto something. One by one I was finding better ways to address people's questions. *But while I was getting to the infor-mation faster, the readings were going on for hours.* I was determined to give people the *wowest* experience they could possibly have, so I just kept probing and probing. You know me, Curious Kim. I needed to be satisfied myself because I knew that if I was satisfied, my clients would be satisfied too. But the sheer number of readings I was doing, com-bined with their length, was draining me. After completing so many in a single night, I'd feel like I was in a coma the next day. I was knocked out cold. I had to alternate the days when I could take appointments with recovery days.

NEW VENUES

Then one day this gentleman and his wife came to see me. I gave them a great reading and they were very pleased. I didn't know it at the time but he owned a store that sold all angel-related merchandise—angel quilts, statues, jewelry, and car accessories, among other items. The name of the store was Angels in My Pocket, and this man was appro-priately called Angel Bill by his customers. Afterward, he asked me if I would like to come to his store and read on Saturdays between noon and three o'clock. He said that a few other psychics and mediums were doing this already and he found that it helped attract more customers. I ultimately agreed because I thought it would teach me how to bring through the right spirits instantly and how to stay on track. I could train myself with a little timer to give each person a quality reading within fifteen minutes. This way I could help connect even more peo-ple with their loved ones.

I did that for a while and it definitely honed my skills. I also had the longest line of people waiting for me, so I felt at first as if I was giving opportunity to more people. But as I noticed some of the same faces returning week after week, I decided to try a different means of widen-ing the circle of people I could reach.

I began to do Friday night parties. Someone would host a group of eight to ten people in their home, and I would come in to do fifteen- to twenty-minute individual readings. Each new setting for mediums requires a little refining of the process and these parties were no exception.

While I was reading one person, ten others were waiting outside the room. In a way their loved ones were on standby. But all too often, number eight's deceased mom would come through and interrupt number two's reading. I knew the interrupting soul wasn't necessarily meaning to be rude—it's just really hard for some souls to sustain energy for such a long time. So I would find myself calling out into the hallway and asking, "Whose mother is Elisabeth?" or some other such question in order to give that soul a chance to connect with her daughter while she still could.

I had heard about other mediums who were approaching these house parties differently. Instead of conducting fifteen-minute one-on-one readings for every guest, as I was doing, they would conduct group readings. I knew this was the solution to conserving both my energy and the spirits'. It made more sense to allow them to speak up whenever they needed to. Having their loved ones present in the room the entire time was much better than me having to go outside to summon them.

I had never done this type of group reading before, but my good friend Pat offered her home to me so I could try it out. She invited ten people she knew who were willing to be the guinea pigs. The group reading was a total success and more enjoyable for everyone because the sitters were able to benefit from one another's readings as well as their own. Even I couldn't believe the information that was filtering through.

After this, I quickly learned that in group settings my guides would have to intervene more. So I asked them to help set up the spirit gathering space like a theatrical stage. Then I asked them to tell all those waiting to talk to a loved one to stand behind an invisible curtain until they were called. When I was ready, my guides were to usher members of one family at a time to the center of the stage where I could focus solely on them. The spirits that were "on," so to speak, would enter from the wings. Members from the mother's side of the family came from the left while members of the father's side of the family joined from the right so it was easy for me to identify exactly whom I was speaking with and so everyone could have a turn to talk. Things got much better.

SOME PEOPLE NEVER CHANGE

For the most part, these house parties were rewarding experiences. As it happens, though, not every spirit who speaks out of turn does so because she can't sustain her energy for very long. Sometimes it's just because she never had great manners to begin with. Maybe before she passed away, she was the kind to cut in line at the grocery store too. I used to think that once we got to heaven we'd be holy—we'd take on these saintly characteristics. You know, we'd be way more Godlike. But that isn't what happens at all. Lots of spirits still maintain their quirky personalities.

I discovered this in a big way during one of my very first readings. It was when I was helping out a woman who was an acquaintance at the time but who has since become a good friend. This young woman's uncle lived in New Mexico while she and her mother lived in New York. After the uncle passed away, the circumstances of his death remained a mystery, though this friend and her mother had a few theories about what happened. Given the distance, it wasn't easy for them to follow up and investigate on their own, so they decided to invite me over one day to see what they could find out through Spirit. This man immediately came through using such profanity that I paused for a minute. I'm no prude, but he shocked even me. Every other word out of his mouth was an F-bomb. When I tell you he exhausted every known variation of that curse and then some, I'm not kidding. He was a real man's man—covered almost completely in tattoos from what I could see. His language was so off-color I didn't feel like I could repeat what he was saying. But he did manage to get my attention when he said something that implied his wife had him murdered. He didn't tell me outright, but he showed it to me as if it were a movie. He was standing in his living room while his wife was off in the next room talking to another man in private. Before I knew it, the uncle was hit in the head, knocked unconscious, and dragged into the garage. I even saw the wife and the other man put him into a car and turn the engine on so it would appear as if he had killed himself by asphyxiation through carbon monoxide. I let the family know what I saw and confirmed for them that their loved one *absolutely* did not kill himself. "It was his wife and there was insurance money involved," I told them, because I saw that too. Then I said, "I'm so, so sorry I cannot repeat to you what your brother said to me. He has the filthiest mouth I ever heard." Once I said that, these two women started laughing. Not only were they in stitches, but they were crying. They were laughing and crying at the same time. I had no idea what was happening. The mother couldn't catch her breath. Then she finally explained, "If you ever met my brother, you would understand why what you just said was so funny. He never completed a sentence without ten F-words in it." And that's when I knew for sure that people's personalities stay intact on the other side. It would be proved to me many, many more times during both private and group readings.

I had another aha moment on this subject some time later, thanks to my guides. I was frustrated one day after a reading because no matter how much I tried to get this spirit to give me more information, he just wouldn't cooperate. Later that day I was on the phone with a friend of mine and we got to talking about a mutual acquaintance at our sons' school. My friend asked, "Is it just me or is talking to her like pulling teeth?" I said, "Oh my God, it can get so uncomfortable sometimes because she doesn't say anything. I feel like I'm talking nonstop, and when I give her an opportunity to chime in she'll just listen or give me one-word answers." I really didn't think anything of the conversation until I was mediating later that afternoon. That's when my spirit guide reminded me of what I had said earlier. "Kim, just like that woman on the school committee, some people are fabulous communicators in life and they will still be fabulous communicators in death. And then there are people who are real introverts. It will always be like pulling teeth with them. So it is with the spirits." I instantly thought, "Of course, of course. I'm dealing with lots of different characters. These spirits are still *real people*. I have to remember that." This put my mind at ease and took a lot of pressure off me. I no longer felt like I had to carry on the conversation when the spirit didn't want to. Now, instead of blaming myself for not getting the information flowing, I simply say, "Geez, this guy is quiet," or "This is a woman of few words."

OCCUPATIONAL HAZARD

Since these readings could get overwhelming sometimes, I'd take a moment before each one to ask for help. I would say, "Spirit, please give me the words this person needs to hear. Let me be a clear channel with an open heart. Allow me to deliver healing messages—ones that serve the highest good for all concerned. Help me to reserve judgment and always put aside my ego so I can be a pure, clean voice for you." By the end of most readings, I found that I was healed a bit too. As I reassured someone that their loved one was safe and sound on the other side, I reinforced to myself that there really is another place we go to after this one. And that thought would bring me peace.

But for as many days as my heart would sing after a reading, there were days when I couldn't see the lighter side of life. Some readings would stay with me for days—even weeks—the way a sad movie does. I couldn't shake them. I would sometimes feel a form of survivor's guilt. If I was going to a barbecue I would think about that mother who was home crying over the loss of her son. There were no neighborhood parties for her. There was no joy at Christmastime for her. I was taking people's pain on as my own, and I recognized that it was not healthy to do this.

Sensitive people, and people who do healing work of any kind, especially mediums, need to consciously and proactively take measures to keep themselves well, physically and emotionally.

I already mentioned how depleted my energies would get after a long day of back-to-back readings or after a house party or large group events. That's because in addition to absorbing other people's grief and a host of other emotions and energies, I am also raising my vibrations on demand, and frequently determining a spirit's cause of death by experiencing it in my own body. Remember how I said some spirits will make me feel their heart attack as if it is happening to me? How I will lose my breath when someone has passed of lung cancer? How my body can feel the impact of a bullet or an oncoming car or train? The physical toll of this work is just as strong as the more obvious emotional toll. To help you understand this I have to explain more about the chakra system within us all—a system mediums rely on heavily.

Chakras

As I mentioned briefly in chapter 2, there are seven main chakras that serve as psychic organs producing and distributing energies throughout your being. Their location and their more general functions are as follows:

1. The first is the Root chakra, located at the base of the spine in the general tailbone area. It is what helps us feel stable, grounded, and secure.

2. The second is the Navel or Sacral chakra, positioned in the lower abdomen, just below the navel. It is what feeds our passions and creativity.

3. The third is the Solar Plexus chakra, found just above the stomach and just below the chest or diaphragm. It is what drives self-determination and willpower—that fire in our belly.

4. The fourth is the Heart chakra, located in the middle of your chest by your breastbone. It is what enables us to love and to heal ourselves and others through that same love.

5. The fifth is the Throat chakra, residing directly under your chin in the middle of your throat. It is what promotes communication—our listening skills as well as our self-expression.

6. The sixth is the Brow chakra, also known as the Third Eye. It sits on the forehead directly between your two eyebrows. It is what grants us insight, awareness, and heightened perception.

7. The seventh chakra is the Crown chakra, and it is located at the top of the head. It is what provides *knowing*—a oneness or synchronicity with the Universe.

Most people are unaware of their chakras, which is why these organs remain inactive and their intuitive and psychic abilities stay largely underdeveloped. It is believed that if your chakras and the energies that travel through them are grounded and well balanced, then you will live a life that is grounded and well balanced too. Likewise, if your chakras and energies are blocked, so too will your health and progress be blocked until those chakras can be cleared and their energies balanced.

The more specific psychic abilities associated with the chakras are roughly as follows:

When the Root, Sacral, and Solar Plexus chakras—collectively called the *Lower Three Chakras*—are awakened, they are associated with what is known as *psychism*. Psychism includes such abilities as channeling, telepathy, precognition, and dreaming (yes, dreaming is considered a psychic ability since the dream state is a crude form of astral projection!).

When the Heart, Throat, Brow, and Crown chakras—collectively called the *Four Higher Chakras*—are awakened, they produce psychic abilities involving the more conscious use and control of one's gifts.

The awakening of the Heart chakra produces enhanced empathic abilities and the ability to heal.

- The awakening of the Throat chakra leads to clairaudience, which is the ability to hear on the nonphysical planes with your spiritual ears.

- The awakening of the Brow or Third Eye chakra, leads to clairvoyance, or the ability to see on the nonphysical planes.

- And the awakening of the Crown chakra leads to becoming an open channel and provides the ability to consciously travel on nonphysical planes to unite with the collective pool of consciousness, ultimately leading your soul to awaken to its true nature.

Although many mediums will say that they "close themselves off" after readings to signal to other spirits that they are now off duty, the Crown chakra is never fully closed. It is either open, in the process of opening, or blocked. The easiest way for you to tell if your Crown chakra is blocked is if you have a lack of faith. People who live without hope or who feel as if they have to do this thing called *life* alone usually do not connect to a higher source. But awakening the Crown is always possible when you balance the other six energy centers. Sometimes it opens spontaneously when someone is in a crisis. For instance, when something really terrible is happening, people have been known to call out God's name spontaneously. This deep desire to appeal to God (or unconditional love) is evidence of the connection our soul has to Spirit from birth. When we get closer to the Source, God, or All That Is, the opening of the Crown chakra is the natural result.

The Crown chakra is used to bring more light into your being so you can evolve spiritually; when you are a medium, it is also the point through which the energy of the spirit whose message you are delivering enters. This energy passes through the spine, which connects to each of the seven chakras. The psychic organs then apply their specific awakened abilities to help read and communicate these messages.

As you can imagine, a lot of energy has passed through my spine over the years. I have done thousands and thousands of readings and I like to joke that I have the backache to prove it. A few years ago I needed surgery to relieve the pain caused by a hereditary condition called spinal stenosis. I consulted with five different doctors. After each one looked at my X-rays they couldn't believe how many directions my disks were going in. The disks looked as if they were pushed out of alignment. I was asked if I was in a car accident. One surgeon told me that parts of my spine looked like that of a seventy-year-old woman while other parts looked young and healthy. Although I fully understand that this condition is genetic and I have no evidence to the contrary, I still wonder how much of a role all that energy flowing through my spine played in giving me so many back problems.

Again, anyone who is sensitive to the energy around them, or engaged in doing healing or light work of any kind—especially mediums and prospective mediums—should learn to cleanse their chakras, ground and balance their energies, and raise their vibrations!

Nothing a Little Chakra Therapy Can't Help!

There are so many fun and meaningful ways to help support your chakra system. Here are a few of my favorites along with some basics everyone should know.

• *Add color to your life!* Think of the chakra system as seven spinning wheels of light constantly in motion, dispersing energy. Every living being emits some of this subtle energy around their physical outline in the form of an aura. Auras can extend anywhere from a few inches to as far as two to three feet. There are seven different chakras, each associated with a specific color that can be seen in the different layers of the aura. (Note that the color of the aura can change often, depending on your mood. Since your energy field can spill over into other people's auras, and vice versa, you may find yourself reacting to other people's moods or emotions. It can be tricky knowing the difference between your thoughts and emotions and those of other people. If you find your mood changes on a dime, take notice of who is around you.) The colors associated with each chakra are as follows:

> The Root chakra's color is red.
> The Navel or Sacral chakra's color is orange.
> The Solar Plexus chakra's color is yellow or gold.
> The Heart chakra's color is green.
> The Throat chakra's color is blue.

The Brow or Third Eye chakra's color is indigo or dark blue.

The Crown chakra is violet or purple.

One great way to help balance and support the energy of a chakra is to wear its corresponding color. You can also add accents of that color to your home or office decor and eat foods that naturally come in that color too. Absorbing colors' energy is very uplifting.

- *Let Mother Earth help.* Many crystals and stones contain energies that can support your chakras as well. While the colors of these stones can often guide you to the right choices, I've listed some of the most effective pairings below. When you wish to support a particular chakra, place the crystal I've matched it to in your home or office, carry it in your pocket, or wear it as jewelry. You can even lie down and place one or all seven of them on their respective chakras as you meditate. As you support your chakras in this way, look for improvements to other related functions as I describe them here.

    Use red jasper to support the Root chakra. It is also good for increasing courage, protection, justice, sexual desire, and circulation as well as for unblocking energy and combatting anemia.

    Use carnelian crystal to support the Navel or Sacral chakra. It also helps boost energy and creative thinking, relieves depression, and aids in treating infertility, asthma, poor digestion, and kidney problems.

    Use golden quartz to support the Solar Plexus chakra. It also helps ease anxiety and panic; promotes personal power, mental clarity, energy, and flexibility; and aids in digestion.

Use green aventurine to support the Heart chakra. It also helps to promote healing; attract money and career success; maintain healthy hair and skin; relieve acne, allergies, headaches, and inflammation; and support the lungs.

Use lapis lazuli to support the Throat chakra. It also helps release old attachments and grief, lowers blood pressure, supports the throat, and promotes peace and greater comfort with public speaking, as well as helps with the resolve to break bad habits.

Use amethyst to support the Brow or Third Eye chakra. It helps to align and heal ailments of *both* the sixth and seventh chakras, opens and heightens spiritual and psychic awareness, possesses calming qualities, eases stress, and enhances perspective and introspection. This is an especially powerful tool in increasing intuition and psychic development. When used to support the Third Eye chakra, which is the energy center for all levels of consciousness, amethyst assists in the transition from a normal state of consciousness to a state of deeper awareness.

Use clear quartz to support the Crown chakra. It helps increase intuition and connects you with the Divine Mind. It is especially useful when meditating and for allowing messages to filter through with clarity and ease.

While you are connecting with Mother Earth this way, also consider hugging or standing flush up against a tree or gardening, as trees and plant life transmute energy all the time. In the same way that they purify the air, they help purify your chakras. They not only cleanse our energies, but ground them too. The same can be said for showering and swimming!

- *Dance to your heart's content.* Moving around ensures that your energy remains in motion and that whatever is blocked is quickly unblocked. The music you dance to can send out good vibrations too.

- *Practice yoga or Tai Chi.* These exercises can serve the same purpose as dancing. They help remove blockages, allowing energy to flow more freely throughout your body.

- *Enjoy a good belly laugh.* Laughter is contagious. It is one of the easiest ways to spread positive energy. It really does *lift your spirits.*

- *Let your love shine brightly.* Give and receive as much love as you can. There are many different kinds of love to enjoy and extend. It's okay if you haven't found your soul mate yet. Help a neighbor, be a good friend, or volunteer for a cause. Caring for a pet promotes unconditional love too. Don't hesitate to accept the affections they offer in response to yours.

- *Treat your body like a temple.* Avoid the things that deplete your energy including lack of sleep, toxic chemicals, negative thinking, and stress. Embrace positive thinking and eating natural, organic, and locally grown foods. Enjoy massages, saunas, and other quick pick-me-ups.

- *Spend more time with family and friends.* Setting boundaries with outside influences, such as work and social obligations, and surrounding yourself with loved ones naturally create a balance of energy in your life.

- *Engage in prayer and meditation.* Planned daily meditation and spontaneous meditation can both help draw positive energies to you and distance you from negative ones. Sometimes we can't help but stand next to someone who has had a bad day or who may be holding on to resentment or anger. If you ride a crowded subway or bus on your daily commute, or if you've ever found yourself in line at the grocery store behind an angry shopper, you know what I mean. One of the quickest and easiest ways I've found to activate your chakras, remove unwanted energy from your aura, and help raise your vibrations is to follow the simple meditation below. Remember, meditation does not need to be a huge ordeal or take up much of your time. It can be done anywhere and as often as you deem necessary. The more you do it, the clearer your chakras and the stronger your aura will be.

The Good Vibrations Meditation

• It is best to be in a comfortable position with your feet touching the ground and your head slightly lifted toward the heavens. You can stand or sit, whichever you prefer. (Note: Being barefoot will help better ground you to the earth.)

• Close your eyes and take a few deep, cleansing breaths. First breathe in through your nose, then exhale through your mouth. Do this three times.

• Imagine that you are outside on a beautiful clear day and the sun is shining brightly upon you.

+ In your mind's eye, picture the golden sun and its powerful rays entering you through the top of your head. As the rays move downward, this brilliant light fills your forehead where your third eye is located. You are now able to see clearly what has been hidden from you in the past. This light is slowly moving into your Throat chakra, opening up any blockages that may have prevented you from speaking your truth. Next, feel the warmth of the sun seeping down into your chest and into your Heart chakra. You see a ball of spinning light enter as it opens up your heart to receive more love. You are now letting go of any anger or resentments. Your body feels less weighty knowing that this light is washing away any negativity. You're intuitively aware of every cell in your body being rejuvenated, making you whole and new. Feel the golden rays penetrate farther down to the space just above your navel, into your solar plexus, leaving you feeling powerful, confident, and strong. As every nook and cranny is filling up with this pure light, feel it as it overflows into your Sacral chakra, below your navel. You are now allowing yourself to let go of the old to make room for the new. Know that these are necessary changes that will drive you closer to finding your life's purpose. Allow yourself the freedom to experience happiness like never before. Your soul is waking up to its true destiny. As the light moves down into the base of your spine, it is activating your Root chakra. You feel as if you are wrapped in a warm blanket keeping you safe and secure. You are feeling stable and balanced. As the sun's energy enters both of your legs, you look down and notice this brilliant light has descended under your feet and down into Mother Earth, transmuting it into a cleansing, healing ball of light that shoots up high until it's around your crown, showering you in a waterfall of sparkling, divine energy. You feel a slight tug at the base of your spine, grounding you to the

> earth, making you feel at one with the Universe. There is no room for any fears or insecurities. You are safe, secure, and unconditionally loved. Know that you are fully protected and nothing negative can harm you. Your vibrations are now raised and you are feeling more alive and vibrant. You are a special child of the Divine. You may now open your eyes and give thanks.

Many of you may remember that during Tatum O'Neal's episode of *The Haunting Of...* I was compelled to give her the heart-shaped rose quartz I always carried with me. It was a special stone. You will recall that when I once regressed Anthony, my grandmother came through and told me to keep an open heart. Rose quartz has the power to help you do that. I didn't mention the rose quartz stone earlier, but it is one of the more powerful ones to keep in mind. It does more than bring romantic love into your life—it brings divine love, self-love, and a love of life and living. It really does invigorate the energy force within you and readies you for receiving every kind of love there is. I guess that's why I just love this particular type of stone.

As for the episode with Tatum, talk about leaving an encounter completely drained! There were so many different kinds of energy swirling around that day—the loving energy Tatum brought with her for her son, and the healing energies her mother and Farrah Fawcett brought through for her, all set against the harsh energies of a spirit couple battling it out nonstop in the kitchen and some of the energy still left with Tatum from past traumas. I couldn't move for days after that. I found myself saying a special meditation for her. She has made so many efforts to transmute all the negative experiences in her life into something positive that I concentrated on the transformative power of energy and willed strong healing winds of change her way.

As you can see, I really do use these healing practices in my life and in my work all the time. Over the years I have learned much from Spirit to help turn the chaos of a thousand spirits talking to me at once into a meaningful dialogue each time I conduct a reading. And I have used countless tools to change and use energies wisely. It really still is amazing to me how many resources the Divine provides to us.

Chapter 10

Spreading Your Wings

Learning Complementary Modalities

So much was going on in my life between the private readings and the house parties that I didn't dare think ahead to the future. I really am someone who tries to live in the moment—in the here and now. I'm guided by that famous old adage: "Yesterday is history, tomorrow is a mystery, today is a gift from God, which is why we call it the present." But when I was a child I did have an intuition of what the future would hold. It was a big joke in my family while I was growing up, and it's still a big joke with us today. I always said to my mother, "I'm going to be on TV, Mommy," and she'd say, "Really?" Then, with the kind of assurance kids naturally have, I would add, "I just know it." Of course my mother would never crush my dreams. What mother would? She and the rest of the family bought into the prospect and started calling me "the movie star." They even nicknamed me Contessa, as if they were already celebrating my fame. The part that strikes me as interesting now, however, is that I *never* said, "I'm going to be a movie star," "I'm going to be an actress," or "I'm going to be a singer." All I said was "I'm going to be on TV." There were plenty of movie stars, actresses, and singers on television at the time but there certainly were no psychics on TV then. I'm sure that's why I chose my words carefully when I made such a big pronouncement of what I saw.

Spirit was clearly guiding me at that age the way Spirit guides me now, and it somehow found a way to put me in front of the right people at the right time to help get my television career started.

In the summer of 2008, a friend of mine brought up my name to Linda Stasi, who was the *New York Post's* television critic at the time and is currently a columnist for the *Daily News*. She's smart and sassy and knows *everyone* in the media business. It also helped that Linda is no stranger to psychic phenomena. She's always had a keen interest in the subject.

What this friend told her—without my knowledge by the way—was that I had a message for her. She graciously agreed to meet me at her office. On that day we went down to the cafeteria for an iced tea and I know that's when I captivated her. During the reading, her best friend came through and told me that Linda had smuggled her ashes out of the country to be sprinkled over a special place Linda knew would please her. Details, such as the *where, when,* and *why* of it all, will remain between Linda, me, and her friend in spirit, but I know you will appreciate the *how* of it. Linda placed her friend's ashes in a baby powder container! Clever, right?

Of course, she was stunned that I would know all of this, because nobody else did. Well, PS: that was the message that made Linda Stasi such a huge advocate for me. She was convinced I needed to have my own show, and she immediately went into action. She hosted a reading party in her home and invited some very influential friends. To say I am forever indebted to her is an understatement. When Linda Stasi says she's going to do something, believe that she will!

The crowd at the party was filled with people from the media and entertainment worlds, most of who were closer to my age. But there was this one guy who stood out more than the others because he was much younger. He looked as if he were in his midtwenties. I was curious to know what had brought him there, but I didn't ask any questions. After all, I was the medium in the room.

When I began the reading, I went around in a circle and provided messages for each person in turn. First, I was drawn to a mother and daughter tandem to deliver a message from a man named "Ed." He wanted them to know he had accidentally overdosed—that he hadn't committed suicide. This was the answer to a question the pair had been seeking for decades. Next, I was drawn to a woman in her early forties. She was a young widower, and her husband was a famous musician. He wanted to tell her that he loved his funeral where thousands showed up to pay their respects, including many famous people in the music industry. And so it went. By the time I got to the young man who had caught my eye earlier, his grandmother Florence came through. She was wonderful. I described her physical appearance, as I could vividly see her standing behind him. So charming, graceful, and forthcoming. "Florence, Flo! Flo!" she was projecting. She gave me all kinds of details about her grandson's life and provided very specific evidence that she was watching over him. For instance, he was about to purchase his first apartment and was a week away from his closing date. This is something neither Linda Stasi nor anyone else in the room knew about. And the first thing out of Flo's mouth was "I'm proud he's getting his own place; he's too old for roommates."

Afterward, having just received career, relationship, and family advice from his grandma, he came bounding up to me and said that he had had a lot of readings in his life but never one like this before. And so it happened just the way you see it in the movies—this generous man got me in to see some executives at A&E and the rest is history.

LIGHTS, CAMERA, ACTION

Almost immediately, I made my first appearance on *Paranormal State* as a guest medium. I had never been on television before, so naturally I was dying inside. None of my prior experiences with Spirit played out before millions of viewers as it would on TV, but despite my nerves I knew I had to follow up on whatever messages I was getting. I had never limited myself or censored what I was told before, and I wasn't going to start then. This was one of those times I had to totally trust my guides to *not* make me look foolish. As always, they had my back. I quickly went from feeling as if I was completely winging it to knowing for sure that they were helping me soar. In a Season 2 episode entitled "Hide and Seek" I entered a 160-year-old Victorian house without a clue as to what to expect. As we would all learn, a mother and her young son recently moved into the home and during a gut-renovation of the place they unleashed some spirits that were causing some real anxiety for them. Flickering lights and the opening and closing of an automatic garage door that had previously been disabled spooked even the contractors working there. Before I arrived, the new owner also told the investigative team gathered there that a shadowy figure had appeared to the boy several times and that the home had been used at one point for bootlegging. The fact that the basement was compartmentalized into lots of tiny concealed spaces with trapdoors seemed to confirm this. She mentioned too that she found a gun behind one of those trapdoors. When I entered the home I instantly picked up on the many different rooms and hiding spaces below my feet as I stood on the first level. I also picked up on the presence of a bearded man with a pipe named George. The sense that many children went there to play and study was also quite strong. I wondered if it had been a schoolhouse at one time. That's when I felt a young girl's spirit try to get my attention. She was frightened, but she managed to tell me that her name was Abby or Abigail. It wasn't clear if she lived there or if she just went there frequently to play. She showed me the crawl space where she entered the basement. She also showed me how no one could find her one day despite everyone frantically looking for her. George had lured her there for a little game of hide and seek. She died in this house. He had killed her and now both of their spirits were stuck there together. The homeowner quickly recalled how she found a spelling tablet, a pair of shoes, a shirt, and some thimbles when she first moved there. These items were tucked away behind one of the doors in a room wallpapered in a pattern that dated back to the 1800s. I could tell from his energy that even if George could leave he was too afraid to. He was sure if he did that his secret would be found out. The homeowner became emotional and her chest began to tighten as I relayed this information. I could see that Abigail was holding on to her for safety. The young spirit's fear was so great that she wouldn't let go until George was finally commanded to leave and we could witness his spirit exiting the space. Research later revealed that a man named George did in fact live in the house between 1923 and 1925 and that at some point he spent time in a state hospital suffering from a nervous disease. The existence of an Abigail was also confirmed but records could not verify her connection to George. There was a lot more information that came to light but not everything we discover while filming can make it into the final cut because of time constraints or technical reasons. However, I ultimately realized that the messages I was receiving from Spirit—whether they aired or not—were meant as much for me as for the audience. It was truly the first time that I could see how all of the abilities I had been developing up until this point were coming together so organically. All along I knew I was building skills in a lot of different areas, but I never saw it working on a scale this big before. It was all so exciting!

Next A&E put me on *Psychic Kids*. Once again, I was an occasional guest medium. I loved that show because I was a psychic kid once too so I could relate to what these children were experiencing. I found that I was really beginning to get the hang of this TV thing as well. Not only was I comfortable with it, I couldn't wait to do even more of it. What I wanted to be in most was a show that involved the exploration of all the different psychic modalities I was interested in.

It wasn't long after that that A&E called me to do *The Haunting Of . . . .* My wish had come true! I loved the concept the minute I heard it because it truly represented the best mix of the different psychic abilities I'd been practicing and refining for years. It was so liberating to no longer resist my gifts the way I once did, and to actually combine and experiment with them in so many new ways!

When I objectively looked back at my long and bumpy ride, I realized that Spirit had led me to learn past-life regression so I could understand the journey of the soul. It then led me to mediumship so I could convey my understanding to other people one-on-one. As my ability to see energy strengthened, I became a medical intuitive too— the same way different spirits would show me how they passed, they would alert me to illnesses in people's auras that were not necessarily being noted by others, so I could advise someone I was reading for to see a doctor about that pesky cough, or to stay out of the sun and have that mole looked at. Some of the readings I have done over the years have truly been lifesavers. I'll never forget the time a woman's deceased dad came through delivering an urgent message. He insisted that she take her mother to get a CAT scan immediately. He kept pointing to his head, saying, "It's in her head." The woman blurted out, "Tell my dad I'm already on it. I have an appointment next week to see why my mom is getting constant headaches." He was persistent. "No, she needs to go immediately, not next week," he said. Sometimes when I deliver a time-sensitive message such as this one, I don't know if the sitter will follow up on the advice given by the spirit, but in this case she did. Not even a week later the woman called to tell me that she took her father's advice from the other side and decided to rush her mother to the hospital immediately. She explained to the doctors that a psychic medium said her mother needed a CAT scan stat. I guess the doctors obliged, knowing that if they didn't follow up, they might be held responsible if something happened. It was later confirmed by the doctor that it was a good thing the woman acted as quickly as she did because her mother had a blood clot on her brain that could have exploded any minute. He said that if she had made one wrong move or so much as bumped her head, it could have been all over. He also said sometimes these clots explode during the sleep state. The doctors performed emergency surgery, relieving the pressure on the brain. They put her on blood thinners, and they continued to monitor her for quite some time afterward. I saw this woman for another reading a year later when she happily reported that her mother was alive and well and headache free. And I've not only had the privilege of delivering lifesaving news—I've had the pleasure of knowing when a new life is imminent too. Nothing is greater than receiving the news that a couple is going to have a baby even though they had been having difficulty conceiving before.

Integrating all of these gifts made me equal parts medium and equal parts healer. It also enhanced the quality of my readings bigtime and prepared me for the path I'm on now. I realized that with each newly developed skill I had to do more than just receive and relay messages. I had to teach and shed light on the things others were still missing. I felt drawn to television because of its broad reach, and to *The Haunting Of . . .* in particular because it was such a good way of replacing fear with the love and understanding I spoke about at the outset of this book.

Beyond extending greetings to the loved ones we miss on the other side and dispelling doubt that there is an afterlife, I felt I had to assure people in a very real and personal way that death is not the end to life. No matter how we are to live our lives this time around, there is always forgiveness, transcendence, introspection, continued growth, renewed purpose, and another opportunity to try again to make it better. And there are always tons of resources at our disposal to help us do that. I truly believe *The Haunting Of . . .* evidences that. The fact that trapped souls are the ones bringing us these messages never ceases to amaze me. It just goes to show that we all have our roles to play.

At the same time I was realizing how my gifts were coming together to form a more complete message, I was also becoming more aware of just how many people wanted to hear that message. Millions of people share my curiosity about the eternal journey of the soul. Sure, my three-year-long waiting list for readings was already hinting at how we all need to be assured that the soul survives physical death, but the sheer size of the television audience interested in this topic was even more eye-opening. Not only were there shows like *Paranormal State*, *Psychic Kids*, and *The Haunting Of . . .* on TV, but there was a whole network dedicated to exploring this issue!

Of course, it took a long time for all the pieces to fall into place for me, so whatever your psychic interests or gifts are, I certainly don't expect them to fully form by the end of this book, this year, or even this decade. And I certainly don't expect the mix of skills you pursue to mirror mine either. There are many other modalities out there to choose from beyond the ones I've explored. *But one truth applies to them all: if you approach your curiosity and study with the understanding that each psychic ability enhances another, your skills will progress more rapidly and organically. And they will definitely expand what you are able to do.*

Recognizing and Expanding Your Own Psychic Potential

The "Clairs" are not only the foundation of psychic abilities, but also a great example of how this phenomenon of one skill enhancing the other works. You will recall that when I first met the Clairs, it felt as if they were all battling one another to get my attention. It was a lot like MMA fighting—it didn't seem like there were any rules. But in retrospect I realize that they were actually all very cooperative with one another. Spirit wanted to get a message to me about my psychic abilities, but because I was actively *ignoring* my gifts, each of the Clairs took turns to see who could land the message first. If you want to have a less dramatic introduction to your abilities, my advice to you is this: *Don't ignore them.* Meet and make friends with your Clairs. They are already present and supporting you in your everyday life. Some are more dominant than others. Which ones are dominant is different for every person, but once you get to know them, you will find that they all have your back and they enjoy working together to enhance your skills in ways you never imagined.

To prove this, let me take you to a place where you can observe several of the Clairs at once: a hotel. I picked this location because I travel a lot and it is one of those places that remind me of how present my Clairs always are. Maybe they don't all show up at once like at a convention, but several are sure to be present on any given trip. I think they are on high alert because they know I'm in new surroundings and I will need their assistance. They are also on high alert because lots of different energies enter and exit hotels every day—energies that can color my experience. Given the size of the rooms in even the most spacious of hotels, it is also a place where other people's energies can be easily absorbed.

So let's say the night before my husband and I leave for our trip, I *instinctively know* something is off. I get a *nagging thought* that maybe I better double-check on my reservations even though I have a confirmation number. I call the hotel, and it's a good thing I do. I'm not in the system for whatever reason, whether human or computer error. But because I called to check, the hotel management is able to give me the last available room. Goody for me, it's a luxury suite, but I am only being charged for a standard as an apology for their mistake. That sense of knowing is *claircognizance* at work!

I'm excited to get to this hotel—I've heard nice things about it but have not been to it before, nor have I checked out the website. My assistant made all the arrangements and said it came highly recommended, but I have no idea what it looks like. However, I imagine the room decor, from the style of furnishings right down to the wall color. I'm certain this hotel has very classical features, but as I enter I find that the look is completely different. It is thoroughly modern. *But my vision is not wrong.* I am told by the bellhop that the hotel just underwent massive renovations. I ask a few questions about its previous style and sure enough, what I was *envisioning* was how it looked before. That is *clairvoyance* at work, probably for no other reason than because I am a highly visual person and these are the things I like to focus on.

When I enter our room, despite my good mood because of the complete attentiveness of the staff and the beauty of the surroundings, I get an anxious feeling. A knot is already forming in my stomach and my heart is beating fast for no apparent reason. I even feel a slight shortness of breath. "Uh-oh, what's this?" I think. I turn on the TV to distract myself and a wave of anger overcomes me just from touching the remote. I don't know who handled it before me, but I sense they definitely need anger management classes. On the way down to dinner with my husband, we smile at the housekeeper in the hall and she tells us, "It's nice to see a happy couple. The people who stayed in the room before you fought the entire time." That would explain the heaviness I *felt* still lingering in the room. That is *clairsentience* at work. Now I am reminded to cleanse and protect myself from other people's energies, which I try to always do when I'm traveling.

The next morning I am preparing for an important meeting. I have my laptop with me, along with some other materials I want to share with the folks attending the meeting. What I'm carrying is not heavy so much as cumbersome. As I get to the elevator I say to myself, "Great, it's only two floors away." That is my internal voice making an observation. But then I hear another voice say, "Maybe you better take the stairs anyway. You don't want to be late." That was an illogical choice considering I was carrying all this stuff with me and the elevator looked to be coming any minute, but when I got down to the lobby and saw an out-of-order sign and a repairman busily at work to fix it, I recognized that voice. It was *clairaudience* at work! Sometimes it's hard to tell which voice is my internal-thought voice and which is my clairaudient voice, but if one of them is telling me to take the option that's less obvious, it's usually a Clair speaking to me, so I try not to second guess them.

I have yet to experience *clairgustance*—the sense of clear taste—in a hotel, so I'll let you use your imagination as to how that one works. As I said, some Clairs are more dominant than others, and this is not one of my stronger ones. But you see how this goes, right? If you have ever had any experiences like this, then you can be assured you are already in dialogue with your Clairs and you just don't realize it. You can call them intuitions, but each has a specific name and they all begin with "Clair."

What I hope this proves to you is that you are all psychic whether you realize it or not. Now imagine how much more psychic you will be if you acknowledge your Clairs' presence in your life but also acknowledge that when they and your other psychic skills work as a team, amazing things can happen, just as they did for me.

The following are exercises that help you get better acquainted with some of the more active Clairs one by one. Have fun trying them at home!

A few important things to note before getting started:

- I have indicated the chakra associated with each Clair you will be meeting. Cleanse this chakra before exercising its partner Clair by using the methods recommended in chapter 9. If your Clairs have been working for your benefit all your life without you even knowing it, can you imagine the energetic residue that remains behind in their supporting chakras? Chakras are a lot like sponges in that the more they are used, the more they absorb other energies, and the more they absorb other energies, the more they need to be cleansed. So please keep this in mind, not just before each exercise, but as you become more practiced in using each Clair as well. It would be good to get into the habit of cleansing your chakras from time to time.

- All of these exercises should be done in a quiet, comfortable space, with no interruptions or distractions.

- You should sit for each one with your feet firmly touching the ground.

- If at any time your mind wanders to your daily to-do list, make a conscious effort to push those thoughts away. Remind yourself that this is a special time specifically set aside for you.

- Finally, take a few deep, cleansing breaths. Now you may proceed.

DO YOU SEE WHAT I SEE?
ACTIVATING YOUR THIRD EYE CHAKRA
AND DEVELOPING CLAIRVOYANCE

To meet and help build a better relationship with *clairvoyance*, which again, is the ability to see clearly, you will need to focus on the TV screen in your mind. You will recall that this is where you receive messages sent to you psychically as opposed to messages sent to you by the ego or your thought process. This is the same screen where visual memories surface, as well as where your daydreams or imagination comes to life.

Because I tend to process visual information quicker than I do information that I hear or read, clairvoyance was one of the first Clairs to blossom during my psychic awakening. If you are not a visual person, don't fret—you can still learn to train your eye on the screen in your mind. You can engage in the simple remote viewing exercises I described on page 110. When you are ready for a more advanced exercise or you want to vary your practice, try the following one.

This alternative exercise involves asking a friend to select photos of places from around the world. They can be pictures of homes you lived in before, vacation spots you visited, or far-off lands you have never, ever been to. Your friend should *not* share his selections with you until after the exercise is over.

Be sure to have a pen and piece of paper in hand.

Then, sitting with your backs to each other, your friend will mentally project the energies of each photo to you one at a time.

Don't think. Just field the images as they are sent to you and jot down or draw whatever you see. If you don't see specifics, simply note the colors and shapes that present themselves. Write down or draw whatever comes to mind. Sometimes you will envision exact objects or scenes. Other times you may draw their correct shapes, or there are times when all you will get are correct colors. I say this is more difficult than the remote-viewing exercise I offered earlier because it focuses on a picture with multiple images rather than on a single item. In both cases, keep in mind that this is a process that will yield improved results with increased practice.

"HEARS" TO YOU!
ACTIVATING YOUR THROAT CHAKRA AND LEARNING TO BETTER RECOGNIZE CLAIRAUDIENCE

Notice that above I said, "Learning to *Better Recognize* Clairaudience." That is because this particular Clair is tricky. It's one of the more naturally active Clairs, so you don't necessarily need to develop this ability as much as you need help distinguishing its voice from your own. Let me explain: One of the ways in which the spirit world—including our spirit guides and angels—communicate their subtle messages to us is through our inner hearing, sometimes referred to as spiritual hearing. When we develop this sense of clear hearing, or *clairaudience*, the Throat chakra—that is, the energy center responsible for communicating back to the Universe and for speaking our truth—is activated. In other words, we have internal conversations with the Universe on a constant basis without even realizing it. We somehow believe that we're just talking to ourselves. Think back to my conversation in front of the hotel elevator. My own voice, which said, "Great, it's only two floors away" preceded my clairaudient voice, which said, "Maybe you better take the stairs anyway. You don't want to be late." Because figuring out the difference between a voice in your head and your own thoughts can be difficult, I didn't recognize this message as clairaudient until I got downstairs and discovered the elevator was broken. In a clairaudient experience, the message may be puzzling to you—you are made to stop and think, "Huh? Why the heck would I hear directions that make no sense?" Newsflash! This voice is *not* coming from you. You are receiving an important piece of information from the Universe. A divine force is trying to make your life easier.

Note, however, that some people have an easier time with clairaudience because they experience it a little differently. In their case, they receive messages through a faint external voice. The most common example is when they hear a deceased loved one call their name to get their attention. Under those circumstances, when the second voice is distinctly that of someone else, it is evident that they are having a clairaudient experience. Most mediums, including me, have the ability to experience this sense both ways. The external voice is most prevalent, though, when I am doing readings. The spirit almost always whispers its name to me so I can relay it to their loved one as assurance that the message they're about to receive is for real.

But if you, like so many others, experience clairaudience only via the voice in your head, aka an "internal voice," the following are some quick and fun exercises that can help you learn to more readily recognize the difference between the clairaudient voice and your own.

The first exercise involves increasing your awareness that these conversations are even occurring. To do this, keep a running log of all your "elevator experiences"—you know, the times when a voice told you to take the less obvious of two paths to help you avoid a challenge. Seeing how frequently this occurs will help you learn to trust that other voice.

The second exercise involves learning how to listen attentively again. We live in a world where there is so much noise that we've grown accustomed to blocking a lot of it out. To tune your listening skills, set aside some time and play instrumental music in an otherwise quiet space in your home. Listen to classical, jazz, world—whatever genre you prefer. After letting the music settle into your body and relax you, pick out the sound of a single instrument and follow its parts until you are hearing just that. Play the piece again, but this time pick a different instrument to focus on. When you listen to the piece without tuning in this way, the sounds converge beautifully and convey a message that you may not consciously process. But when you listen attentively, you can hear what each instrument is saying to you. When you listen to the piece again, I bet you can hear the dialogue that the various instruments—and the musicians—are having with one another. You are now hearing the piece on an entirely different level. You are hearing a conversation with distinct voices. That's how clairaudience works at its best. Your voice and the Universe can almost sound like one, but when you practice listening to the different parts, you can hear and follow the wisdom in the conversation. Some of the most clairaudient people, of course, are musical composers. I think that part of their work comes from a collaboration with the energies, frequencies, and vibrations they've become so attuned to hearing, which is why music can be so uplifting.

I've shared a third exercise, involving automatic writing, in the last section about claircognizance, because clairaudience and claircognizance work together a lot. When you work on one of these Clairs, each benefits.

GETTING TO THE HEART OF THE MATTER
OPENING AND BALANCING YOUR HEART CHAKRA *AND* ACTIVATING YOUR SACRAL CHAKRA TO DEVELOP CLAIRSENTIENCE

Clairsentience is perhaps the most dominant of all the intuitive skills and is mostly associated with feelings and emotions. A good way to understand this Clair is to think of emotions as "E-motions" or "energy in motion." There are energetic signals that are present in the atmosphere, and as our psychic senses become more developed, we become increasingly more attuned to these vibrations. Clairsentience is best developed through two of the seven chakras: the Heart chakra and the Sacral chakra.

Let's address the Heart chakra first. As humans, we are able to feel a myriad of emotions, such as excitement, anger, joy, fear, and compassion. However, the function of our Heart chakra is giving and receiving pure love. This includes self-love and unconditional love. Having a healthy and balanced Heart chakra allows love to flow in and out of us, freely creating a by-product of contentment, peace, joy, forgiveness, and gratitude.

I'm sure you've heard the expression, "Listen with your heart." In order to do this, we must first practice feeling with the Heart chakra to allow us to be more in touch with our feelings. Unfortunately, many people are raised to conceal their emotions. Expressing them is often perceived as weakness or vulnerability. This is especially true for males in our culture. When displaying sadness or empathy for others by crying when they were younger, they may have been told, "Man up" or "Don't be a sissy." If you hear this message often enough, you begin to conform to it. This is how we close down our Heart chakras, little by little. Although you don't want your kindness to be mistaken for weakness, it is still important to keep your heart intact. In order to have a healthier Heart chakra, it is imperative to

- give more love to yourself and to others,
- practice forgiveness and gratitude, and
- demonstrate compassion.

The following exercises are fairly simple and are sure to stimulate what's been lying dormant for too long. There are many other ways to connect with your physical feelings or emotions, but here are a couple to get you started:

Schedule an evening when no one else will be home to join or distract you. Rent or download a tearjerker movie you have been wanting to see but have never watched before. It must be viewed at home where you are free to cry if you want to and where you won't be swayed by the reaction of the audience around you. Dress in your pajamas or sweats so you don't have to interrupt the film to get more comfortable. Prepare snacks if you like, but try not to have any that are so outrageously delicious they become the focus of your night instead of the movie. Keep a box of tissues nearby. Now view the movie. Again, you must do this *alone* so you can feel the full force of your own emotion without any self-consciousness. When the movie is over, take note of how you feel. What are the emotions you are experiencing? What images are coming to mind? What personal connections are you making?

Another exercise is to write an uncensored letter to someone who hurt you (without sending it, of course!). Be as honest with this person as the freedom of never mailing this letter will allow you to be. Let out all of your emotions. This exercise is great because it not only lets you hear how your own emotions sound, but also unburdens you of hurt in the process.

Now for a discussion of the Sacral chakra. Feelings and

emotions do not filter through the Heart chakra only, as I mentioned earlier. They also filter through the second chakra, known as the Sacral chakra. We are all born with primitive instincts, which are meant to help us navigate the uncharted territories in life. Without even thinking about it, most reputable psychics tap into these invisible energetic vibrations on a daily basis, to help themselves and others translate feelings and emotions that aren't easily understood or explained. They usually do this by listening, trusting, and relying on their "gut feelings." Becoming clairsentient enables you to feel other sensations too, such as the chills or the hair standing up on the back of your neck when you sense either a physical or spiritual presence around you. It can also explain a tap on your shoulder when no one else is in the room with you. It can even signal the possibility of danger. As clairsentience is *clear sensing*, it may help you know who is calling you before your phone even rings.

Many psychics who work with the police to help find missing children rely on a form of clairsentience called psychometry, which we addressed earlier in chapter 7. Being able to access the missing person's energetic vibrations as they were absorbed by an article of clothing or jewelry he once wore can give the psychic many clues, including what the missing person's mind-set is or what emotions he is feeling. The details a psychic picks up from such objects can serve as a barometer of either good news or bad.

Tapping into this universal sea of energetic vibrations can also pull your desires directly to you. But be careful what you wish for, as you just may get it—energy does not discriminate, and thoughts are energy. It is important to note that although developing this Clair can be quite beneficial in helping others, it can be a bit of a drag when you are also absorbing other people's thoughts, feelings, and emotions as your own. The definition of *empathy* is the ability to understand and share the feelings of another. Empathy is also the gateway to a wonder-ful emotion known as compassion. With some practice, you will soon be able to distinguish your feelings or emotions from others around you. In addition to the psychometry exercise offered on page 108, the following is an exercise to help you become more clairsentient via your Sacral chakra:

Hold a picture of a person you don't know anything about. Perhaps it is a friend of a friend. As you do this, call upon your psychic feelings and emotions to tell their story. Don't let their smile fool you. Your friend can verify if your story approxi-mates this person's actual story.

BECOMING A KNOW-IT-ALL
ACTIVATING YOUR CROWN CHAKRA TO DEVELOP CLAIRCOGNIZANCE

Claircognizance, the ability to know something and not know how or why you know it, can come out of the blue. When it does, it likely happens because you're connecting with the Universal Mind, absorbing random thoughts that just pop into your head for no apparent reason. This information enters through the Crown chakra at the top of your head. When acti-vated, this chakra can serve as a funnel. In fact, when I am around someone who has her Crown chakra activated, I actu-ally see the shape of a funnel sitting above her head. This is a sure sign that Spirit is able to feed information in whenever the person is ready and willing.

In the same way that it is difficult to distinguish between your own voice and the voice generated by another with clairaudience, it is difficult to distinguish between your own thought and the thought generated by another with claircog-nizance. Through trial and error, however, I have learned to do so mainly by observing the thought. A person's own thoughts are formed via their conscious mind and are usually influenced by the ego. The ego mind will always try to rationalize thoughts based on your frame of reference and typically will try to protect you from harsh disappointments or failures. By contrast, claircognizance occurs when an unbiased thought filters into your conscious mind. It is a thought that is not coming from you, because you have no context for knowing this information. Instead it is coming from a place of higher wisdom. In other words, your thought pattern at that moment had nothing to do with forming this thought. You are, in this instance, merely the observer of the thought rather than the generator of the thought. There are times when you may question why you are thinking this thought or how you even knew it. For example, earlier on I knew that I should call the hotel and check on my reservations, but I didn't really know why. That thought was not my own. It was very likely the thought of my spirit guide, who knew what havoc there would be if I arrived and had no place to stay. Many mediums and channelers use claircognizance when offering information infused into their consciousness by any number of helpers in the higher realms. The information that is available to us is endless, from predictions for the future to many types of warnings. Have you ever finished someone else's sentence simply because you knew what they were about the say? Or have you known when someone is lying to you even though you have no reason to suspect them of lying, except that every fiber of your being knows they are not telling the truth? Creative people and many inventors have a heightened sense of claircognizance, which generates the inspiration for their work. Many will even admit that the idea just came to them.

Please note that even when we sleep, claircognizance may be trying to filter in. Have you ever awakened with an idea so amazing that you just had to act on it? Or with the solution to a problem that's been driving you nuts? If you learn to trust the thoughts generated from claircognizance, you will always be led by your higher mind, your spirit guides, and angels.

To practice recognizing claircognizance, and to help develop it, you can engage in an automatic writing exercise. Have a friend ask you a question. If they know you well enough they may even ask a question they're aware you've been wrestling with for a while. It might also be best if they send you this question via e-mail so you are alone when you set out to answer it. Before you open the e-mail, call upon your guides in the higher realm to help you answer it. Once you open the e-mail and read the question, do not stop to think about the answer. Let your fingers hit the keyboard with an immediate response. Try to keep conscious thought out of your response by just letting the words flow. When you finally reread your answer you may notice that your first few lines or paragraphs are stream of consciousness, but as you practice this exercise more and more, you will start noticing that the latter part of your answer contains insight and clarity on the subject you didn't have before. It may feel like a wider perspective—an aerial view of the problem—has been offered to you, or a path has been put before you to turn your answer into reality. I find that if I meditate to help clear my mind even before reading the question, I can quiet my own thoughts long enough to ensure that there is little to no stream of consciousness in the response once it's written. It is the other voice's reply.

By the way, automatic writing is experienced by people in different ways: some of us hear the outside thought line by line as if it is being dictated to us, but we *think* it too because we are aware of each word as we write it. In this instance both clairaudience and claircognizance are working together to guide us. This is how I experience it. Others just write the message and are aware of what it says only when they read it at the end of receiving it. This is pure claircognizance.

ROME WASN'T BUILT IN A DAY

Again, please remember that the best psychics or mediums take years to practice developing each of their abilities, including their Clairs. Just as it is true with the physical senses that some people have better hearing than vision, it is also true with the metaphysical senses that some people's clairvoyance is stronger than their clairaudience. After you work on activating each Clair separately, notice how they pitch in to help one another complete a message or understand it quicker.

I genuinely hope that your own intuitive and psychic journeys are as fun and spiritually rewarding as mine have been!

Chapter 11

Being Human

LET ME TELL YOU, being psychic can sometimes make the already complicated business of being human even more complicated. There have been times when, like most parents, I wouldn't let my kids go somewhere or do something because I had a bad feeling about it. I couldn't always distinguish if it was a mother's fear or if it was my spirit guides giving me a heads-up. The times I knew for sure, though, were when I felt something I normally didn't. If the feeling was one of doom and gloom, if I couldn't catch my breath because of anxiety, if I actually started feeling grief ahead of time, or if I had a fleeting thought that was too much for me to bear, then I knew it was for real. I've said no to my kids because of those feelings when they've begged to go some-place on one night that would probably have been fine with me on any other night. When they asked, "Why not this time?" all I could say was "Because my gut told me so." I knew how frustrating it was to miss a big event because of one of my intuitions, but I made the judgment call anyway. Many times I never heard about the outcome—I never got confirmation that I was right. But that didn't matter. Maybe nothing bad happened *because* I kept my sons home that night. Maybe my gut decision was what kept them safe. To this day I don't have a clue if some of the bad feelings I've had were actual premonitions that helped our boys avoid danger, if they were the kind of false alarms that condition parents to regularly err on the side of caution, or if they were remnant fears brought with me from a prior lifetime. All three are equal possibilities.

AGE-OLD WORRIES DIE HARD

If you're not sure what a remnant fear is, let me explain.

There are two kinds of fear. There is the kind you develop or are taught, such as a fear of petting dogs because you were bitten by a dog or because your mother was once bitten by one and she's passed that fright on to you by constantly cautioning you to stay away from them.

Then there's the kind of fear you're born with. This is a fear that stays with you from a prior life. Since the soul remembers everything that ever happened to it, it can call up memories from past lives very easily. The ones that seem to be on speed dial are usually the most traumatic ones. These old recurring fears are *remnant fears*.

Even before my son Joseph was out of diapers he showed signs of having this kind of fear. We'd be in the checkout line at the supermarket buying baby formula and he would get all shaky. Imagine being a nervous wreck when you're only a few months old! This happened every time we were ready to pay, but I didn't know why. When he was old enough to talk, I asked him, "Joseph, what's the matter?" His answer shocked me: "We're going to be poor, Mommy. That's a lot of money you just spent." Pardon my language but I was thinking, "What the hell does he know about money? Or about being poor?" He reacted this way throughout his whole childhood. I finally had to stop taking him with me because he was so stressed out. It made no difference to him if I was spending one dollar or a hundred. He was still in a state about it. Even before most kids understand the concept of money he kept asking me, "Are we going to be poor, Mommy? Did you just spend all your money? How are you going to get more money, Mommy?" Finally, I had to say, "Joseph, I have more money than I know what to do with." I basically lied to him. We were financially comfortable, but I had to make him feel like we were set for life. "Don't worry about the money. I have money," I would reassure him again and again.

"Can I see it when I get home?" he'd ask.

We're talking about a twisted situation here. This boy had real anxiety over this issue. And it wasn't a matter of my kid being nervous by nature. He was nervous about this one concern. Years later during a regression, it came out that Joseph was very, very poor in another lifetime. Mystery solved.

Many people have remnant fears, which play out in all kinds of ways. Some have an inexplicable fear of heights. There may be absolutely no reason in their present life to account for it, but the fear is debilitatingly real to them just the same. I have a theory that many morbidly obese people also have remnant fears. Theirs is often a fear of starvation. I suspect that many of them died of famine in a past life or that there was simply not enough food for them to eat. In this lifetime it's as if their soul is stocking up—it can't possibly get enough food to ensure that such a horror won't happen again. There are other reasons too that people put on excess weight, but in extreme cases, I really do suspect it's a soul thing.

I'm personally petrified of the ocean with no other possible explanation for feeling this way in my current lifetime. I respect the ocean—I even have a beautiful view of it from the windows in my new Florida home. But I've had to work at being able to live that close to it. I've chosen to have a place there because it means being surrounded by family, but when I wake up in the morning and look at the water, I can't feel the peace other people who love it do—including my husband and my sister. Sue's practically a mermaid she loves the sea so much. I feel frightened by it because I know that in one past life I died in a tsunami. For years I've had this recurring vision of the ocean swallowing me at some distant time in some distant place. I really want to feel blessed by this view from my home, but I know the other aspect of the ocean and what it can do. The view is not pleasing to me at all. I want to find peace in it, but I can't because I know the ocean is ferocious, scary, and unpredictable.

ALMOST DROWNING IN FEAR

Despite my phobia, my husband and I bought a boat some years back. He and the rest of my family loved the water too much for me not to try to enjoy it too. Lo and behold, I had one of the most traumatic experiences of this lifetime in it.

The craft was small—only twenty-eight feet or so. It was meant to stay in the lakes or the bay of Long Island. It was never meant to go in the ocean. During the first two seasons we had it, we enjoyed making friends at the marina and mostly took it out near where we lived. I was okay if we stayed in the calm waters, and everyone in the family knew better than to take me out into the ocean.

It was the Fourth of July weekend. My oldest son was away playing in a baseball tournament and my middle son was with his cousins at my sister's house, so only Anthony Jr. was with us. We thought we'd try something a little different and headed to Fire Island for the first time. It was farther than we usually ventured but not by too much. We went for only the day and decided to return by six o'clock so it would still be light out. On the way home I noticed that there was a line of boats going in one direction and we were going the opposite way. I told Anthony but he insisted he knew what he was doing. Two seconds later, there was no land in sight. My worst fear was coming true. We were in the middle of the ocean. We missed the peninsula that leads to the inlet and now the waves were pounding us. I mean *pounding* us. We were definitely going to die. I remember thinking, "This is it. We're done." This boat was not meant to be in the ocean and I didn't see salvation anywhere in sight. The waves in the back where Anthony Jr. and I sat were two feet in the air. We were bouncing up and down. My adrenaline was rushing, and I was lying on top of my son so he wouldn't get hurt or fly off his seat. I looked up and couldn't believe what I saw. My husband's whole body was hanging off the boat. He was holding on to the steering wheel for dear life. He was quite husky at the time—he's since lost a lot of weight. I was convinced that if he let go we would have capsized. But thank God, he stayed strong and his instincts kicked in. He managed to maneuver his way back in while I called the coast guard on my cell phone. Before we got disconnected, they told us they couldn't send anyone to help because their boats weren't made for the ocean either. Just then I looked to the right and spotted the beach. I shouted to Anthony and somehow he got us there. In the midst of all this insanity we realized that we had actually landed on a nude beach. I'll never forget my young son's reaction to the few topless women who were still there at that hour. But the really noteworthy reaction that evening was the coast guard's. We called in our position and when they finally arrived by land, because there was no way for them to get to us by water, they told us they were stunned we had survived. They informed us that it was way more dangerous to beach a boat because of the hazards the sandbars posed than to stay out there in the ocean. We managed to avert total destruction only because a massive wave carried us up and over the sandbar. The Coasties had been braced for the worst so when they saw that we were okay, they kept telling us how lucky we were. I said, "Wait, you mean to tell me in all your years you never heard of anyone beaching their boat?" They shook their heads and said, "No. They just don't make it out alive." It was only then that I really understood the magnitude of what happened to us and how we were divinely guided that day.

The point of telling you this story is that I think I'm supposed to get over this fear once and for all. I believe that every life is an opportunity for us to move forward, and my little side trip to the ocean and back again was proof of that. Spirit led me both ways—out into the open water and then safely to shore—to show me it could have ended badly but it didn't.

As I reflect on it all now, I realize I was probably meant to learn this lesson much sooner, and when I didn't, my guides knew they had to clobber me over the head with it. You see, when my kids were very young I didn't want my remnant fears to become their newly developed ones, so I made a conscious effort to avoid that. It was tougher to do than you might think because in the same way that I visualized myself getting swallowed up by water in a tsunami, I also had recurring visions of my children drowning in water. So being the stubborn person that I am, I made it my mission to turn them each into excellent swimmers. They all had lessons with terrific instructors and ample opportunity to practice and get stronger.

My mind wasn't fully at ease, though, until I went with Anthony to Las Vegas on a business trip. We were in an amazing crystal shop in the Luxor Hotel when I noticed a psychic giving a reading to a woman at a small table in the back. As this woman was leaving the store, she told me that she had just had the best reading ever. I thought maybe I should give it a try too. The first thing this psychic asked me was "Are you afraid your children are going to drown?" I couldn't believe she honed right in on this. She made a few other statements that were right on the money and then she proceeded to tell me what my fear was about. "In one of your past lives you lived in Egypt and your children were swept away in a devastating flood that ran right in front of your eyes. You could not save them," she said. I was flabbergasted. That matched the recurring vision I had of my children drowning. Whereas I was always focused on their faces as they were going under, her account broadened my perspective to show me where it happened and *when*. She continued, "Now that I told you this you're not going to have this fear anymore. It's not from this life. It will never happen in this life."

When I think about both of these events together—my drowning at sea in one lifetime and my witnessing the drowning of my children in another lifetime—there is no doubt in my mind that many of our fears were born in another time and place, and that's probably where we should leave them.

MY PACT WITH SPIRIT

Just as it often helps to know things about our past lives, it sometimes helps *not* to know things about our present one. I came to this conclusion when I first became a medium and saw the pain that many people endure when their loved ones are dealing with a prolonged illness. It is horrible to know a person's fate in advance and then have to watch it unfold over a long period of time. In order to continue doing my work and remain a Happy Medium, I decided I didn't want to know how my loved ones would pass any sooner than I would know if I didn't have this gift. In fact, I asked that I *not* know these kinds of details for anyone. I'm not sure if this is a pact God made with just me because I asked or if it's one that is extended to all mediums, but either way I'm grateful for it.

There was one time, though, when not knowing was devastating. My sister's husband, Jack, was more than a brother-in-law to us; he was a soul brother. Just like I've been saying all along about picking your family to help serve a purpose in your life, we picked Jack or he picked us for lots of reasons that later turned out to be great blessings. He was the kind of guy who was good at everything he did. He was a loving husband and father and he provided for his family in true style. He owned a beautiful mansion on seven acres of land in Old Westbury, one of Long Island's most coveted communities. He was a successful entrepreneur by the time he was twenty-one, he had a black belt in karate, he was a pilot who logged more miles than I can count, and he owned his own plane.

Anthony never had a brother before Jack, and Jack never had a brother either, so it was natural that they lived up to this role for each other. Jack was always offering guidance in any way that he could. He helped us buy our first house because he wanted us to move closer to him and my sister. We would go to their place every weekend so the kids could play in the pool and enjoy their cousins' company the way I grew up with my cousins. We even vacationed together. We always had so much fun.

One thing to note about Jack is that he always faced his fears. Although I'm telling you all about the things that frightened me to help make a point, I'm generally not held back by my fears, big or small. As you've seen, fear didn't keep me out of the water. But Jack's plane was a different story. I really didn't like it. I had confidence that he was a good pilot. That wasn't my concern. I never had any visions that suggested it was a past-life thing. That wasn't it either. Just something about his plane never sat well with me.

My feeling was so strong that one day after Jack took my husband up for a ride I made Anthony promise me he would never get in that plane again. He knew from my tone of voice that I wasn't kidding around.

Shortly after that, my parents announced they were selling their home and moving to Florida. They intended to be snowbirds, spending the cold winters down there and the warmer seasons in New York. Or at least that was the plan: when moving day came, they were going to drive to Florida in their own car, a moving truck was going to follow with their furniture, and Jack decided he was going to fly there too because his sister just had a baby and he thought he would visit her and check out my parents' new place at the same time. The trip was scheduled for August 30, a little less than two weeks before school was starting. My son Joseph and my niece Maria thought it might be nice to end the summer in Florida with their grandparents, so they planned on going too. My sister couldn't go because she was getting her oldest child ready for college. Jack offered to take Anthony in the plane, but when I heard that, I flipped out. I said, "Did you really think I was kidding when I asked you to make that promise?" His response was classic—just the kind of thing I should have expected him to say— "When it's my time, it's my time. Whether I die in a plane or a train, it doesn't matter. I could die crossing the street." He had just bought a motorcycle so I quickly reminded him that if he went against my wishes on this, between the Harley and the plane, he was definitely increasing his odds. I would have said anything to keep him from getting on that plane. I had never been as serious in my entire life: "Read my lips. If you get on that plane, I promise you when you get home you will find divorce papers on the table." That landed hard. Those were words neither of us ever said to each other—and never even thought. If I was threatening that, he knew I meant business. He told Jack he couldn't go. Jack then called three other buddies who for one reason or another couldn't join him either. A fourth finally agreed, and having two more seats available in the plane, Jack offered to take Joseph and Maria too. If it wasn't for my son's and Maria's love for road trips, and my father's genius idea of putting comfy couches in the back of his van, the kids might have tried to convince me (unsuccessfully, of course) that a two-hour plane trip was better than an eighteen-hour car ride, but as it was they chose to go with their grandparents and looked forward to the adventure of it all.

Just before Jack got on the plane that morning he gave me a call. As much money as he had, he was always looking for a deal and he knew I was too. We had that in common. He was always on a quest and I was always on a budget.

"Hey, Kim," he said. "Did you see the circular at the market today? Chicken cutlets are $2.99 a pound."

"Get out of here. That's amazing. I'll have to pick some up."

Then he joked, "When am I going to get you in my plane? You're the only one who's never been."

I don't pull any punches so I said, "You're never going to get me in your plane, Jack."

"Why? Don't you trust me?" he asked.

"I trust you, but I don't trust the plane, so stop asking. Don't ever ask me again. I don't like going in regular airplanes; I'm not going in yours."

"Oh for God's sake," he said, and then he just laughed.

There was one more thing he wanted to ask his kindred deal buddy.

"Listen, Kim. Can you do me a favor?"

"What?"

"I have all our airline tickets booked for February."

(We had all taken a fabulous vacation to Cancun together a few years earlier—me, Anthony, my parents, Sue, Jack, and all of the kids. It was the trip of a lifetime and we were all hoping to catch magic a second time, if that was even possible, during the upcoming winter break.)

"I need you to check every day if the fare goes up or down because when it goes down we've got to lock in that price."

He could have asked Sue to do this, but knowing Jack, he was trying to take one more thing off my sister's to-do list to help lighten her load, and make sure Anthony and I didn't overpay for the tickets either.

"All right. Consider it done."

Then he said something I can't believe I didn't pick up on sooner.

"You have to promise me if I die you'll get to Cancun."

"What? If you die, you think I'm going to Cancun? Are you nuts?"

"Promise me, Kim, you'll all go. Promise me you'll all get there."

I said, "Jack, I'm not promising anything. That's the most ridiculous thing I ever heard in my life."

And with that he said, "Good-bye, but just keep an eye on those airline tickets."

Later that night, Anthony and I were at a comedy club in the city. I didn't know why, but Jack kept coming to mind. I wasn't worried or anything. He was just in my thoughts. At about eight thirty the next morning I woke up with this overwhelming craving for cannoli. I got dressed and it was like I was on a mission. I was headed to the bakery when I got a call from my sister.

"Kim, Kim, Jack's dead."

"What?"

"I know he's dead," she said, crying into the phone.

"What do you mean?"

"He didn't call me. He should have called me when he got to Florida. I don't know what to do. I'm calling the police."

"Don't worry," I told her. "I'll be right over. But whatever you do, don't jump to any conclusions."

Because of my crazy cannoli craving I was in the car headed in the direction of her home and almost there already.

Since my husband, Anthony, loves to listen to Howard Stern, the radio in the car was set to SiriusXM. Howard and Robin were doing the news when Robin said, "Oh Howard, a small plane went down over a campus in Lexington, Virginia. It didn't hurt anybody but the pilot died."

Would you believe it still didn't dawn on me? I got to my sister's house quickly and was headed up the long winding driveway when I saw the state trooper. I could see Sue was hysterical.

It was confirmed. Jack was dead. His body had been identified. Among the debris they had found a surgical steel rod that had been placed in his leg to mend a bad fracture a number of years ago, and that helped the authorities make the connection. His friend John perished too. Aviation called the local police station, and since my sister had already placed a missing person report, they came directly to deliver the news to her. When I heard what they were saying, it clicked. I thought aloud, "It was in Lexington, Virginia."

"How do you know?" Sue asked.

"It was just on Howard Stern."

Even with my naturally heightened senses I missed the clues. All the red flags were there and I didn't notice a single one of them. I couldn't understand how that happened. At that moment I wasn't thinking about my pact with God not to show me anyone's death.

I do sometimes wonder, though, if Jack had a premonition when I didn't. Reflecting upon the end of our conversation that morning, I suspect he might have.

My psychic abilities only kicked in again as we got closer to the funeral service. Then, just like what happened in celebration of Uncle Nunzio's life, a poem was dictated to me in part by Jack and in part by God. It read like this:

I Did Not Leave Completely

Although it's been a little while since I've seen you last,
There is so much that I must say about our treasured past.
There are so many memories that time will not erase,
They'll stay embedded in your heart until we're face-to-face.
I didn't mean to go so soon,
But I had no other choice.

I did not leave completely.
Can't you hear my voice?
I'm never far away from you,
I'm always in the way.
I'm with you when you're sleeping
And as you go about your day.

Please don't think I left you.
That will never be.
I have to help on this side.
Now they depend on me.

I asked the Lord a question.
Why did he need me here?
He looked at me, and smiled and said, "Now I'll tell you dear.
You've done so much in little time and passed the many tests,
You listened and you helped me carry out my many quests."

I told him that I couldn't leave,
I had too much left to do.
He told me that I had to go.
"Now they'll depend on Sue.
They're stronger than you think they are,
You've taught them very well.
They'll use what you have taught them, you'll see
Time will tell.

"He did not leave completely,
He'll always be around.
He did not leave completely,
He's with me safe and sound."

MAKING SENSE OF LOSS

As my sister knows all too well, the most painful experiences are ones that teach us the most about ourselves—about our strengths and our vulnerabilities, about our purpose and our plan. It's in times like this that the unexpectedness of it all brings us closer to the Divine. In hindsight, I look at this loss and I look at my pact with God and reconfirm that while increasing our understanding and connection to the spirit world can help us live freer, more purposeful, less fearful lives, nothing can spare us from death or from the lessons we are meant to learn while we're here—lessons we had a strong hand in picking. Our guides can direct and protect us up to a point, but our lesson plan and our exit has been written by us in advance. So while drawing closer to Spirit and increasing your knowledge of what awaits you is important, you still have to live life here on earth according to the mission you agreed to. That goes for psychic mediums as well as anyone else.

In some ways, Anthony was right, although I didn't want to admit it. When it's our time, it's our time. I remember Kali once told me that we get an average of three exit points in life, but that the last exit point is nonnegotiable. And I know she was right. I'm sure that as an adventure seeker, Jack averted death's calling before.

WHAT MORE I LEARNED ABOUT LIFE FROM FEAR

Caution, which is sometimes mistaken for fear, has a practical purpose in the ego world. It can help us develop commonsense practices for dangerous situations. But what is interesting about the kind of fear we have been talking about here is that it is rooted in the unknown—in what still remains dark to us. Our greatest fear is death. We don't have just fear of starving; we have fear of starving to death. We don't have just fear of heights; we have fear of falling to our death. And so on and so on.

But when we understand that death does not represent the end but rather a continuation, when we comprehend that it's not lights out but that it's light on, when we know beyond a shadow of a doubt that we will see our loved ones again and that this earthly life is merely a stopover on a never-ending journey of our soul, only then can we begin to dispel fear and embrace love.

Transmuting the Energy of Fear into Love

Because fear blocks energy, it can cause so many problems in people's lives. It can dim your aura more than any other known toxin. That is why you must do all you can to rid yourself of it. The exercise I developed for myself can be described in one step, but it's nowhere near as easy as the other exercises I offer in this book. Take the time to do it anyway and I promise it will be the most powerful exercise of them all!

The trick, believe it or not, is to embrace the fear. Decide that you want to do something about it—that you want to turn its negativity into something positive (I'm thinking maybe *love* or *enlightenment*). Remember what I did when facing my fear of the open water? I tried to create new and happier memories surrounding that fear. I bought a boat with my husband and enjoyed lots of leisurely afternoons on it. We had so many good times with family and friends because of that choice. Even if one of those afternoons was truly scary, all those other afternoons managed to help me chip away at the bad associations I previously had of the ocean. Even if I never manage to fully replace the old associations with better ones, I will have at least nudged them out of the way a little. I'm doing the same thing right now with my new condo in Florida. I chose to be surrounded by ocean because in this case it also means being surrounded by loved ones. I have lots of family there whom I missed once they relocated. Again, I hope to make new memories to replace the ones I had of the ocean before. In each of these acts I am choosing love over my remnant fear, and you can too. Just be sure, when you make these choices, to bring along sensitive, supportive, and mindful people whose presence will help you rewrite your experience of whatever it is you fear.

Chapter 12

Fulfilling Your Destiny

> *Living Life in Love and Light*

WHENEVER PEOPLE ASK ME how psychic mediumship works, I always tell them it's a lot like reading a book—I can open to a page in their lives and scan straight through. I do this with their permission, of course; otherwise it's no different than rifling through their drawers, closets, or refrigerator. But basically that's what I do. *I read people's energy*—their soul energy.

As I sat down to complete this final chapter, I realized that by writing this book I had invited you to have a similar experience. Reading *The Happy Medium* is a lot like reading *my energy*. So far you've peeked into my present and past lives. You've witnessed my struggle over how my gifts fit into my soul's purpose. You've seen how I learned all about the other side. You've heard several conversations with spirit guides and master teachers. And hopefully you've seen evidence along the way that each life we live presents a new opportunity to fulfill our destiny.

But if you're anything like I was at this same stage of seeking answers, you probably still have a few more questions. So let's take a minute to review.

When you first hear about soul contracts, it sounds like everything in life is predetermined—what you will learn here, who you will learn it with, where you'll live, and what your social status will be is all decided in advance. Even your exit point (aka your physical death) is preset.

When you learn about free will you realize that it was *you* who helped preselect those terms for yourself on the other side and that it's also *you* who gets to decide if you will live by them on this side based on the choices you make. Your guides can help you but they cannot interfere with free will. Remember they have a strict hands-off policy they have to follow on this subject.

When you finally put two and two together you realize that every right choice you make with your free will can get you closer to fulfilling your destiny, while every wrong choice can end up delaying the fulfillment of your life goals.

Now this is where it gets tricky. If we're not consciously aware of the terms of our contract, then having all the free will in the world is a lot like shooting in the dark. The big questions that start swirling in your head are *What will it take to get closer to the light?* And *What do I do to get another look at that contract?*

I have faith in you. I know you know the answers already, but let me help break it down for you.

Hint #1: It takes more than functioning with the ego mind to see the ethereal energy your contract is written on. You can't hope to fulfill your destiny or to attain Enlightenment if you see the world through only your five senses. You have to develop your heart mind—the sixth sense that draws you closer to the light so you can see the less visible workings of the Universe and so you can get another look at the terms of your soul agreement.

Hint #2: In the world of energy, fear leads to darkness and love leads to light. Learning to use your heart mind—your sixth sense—is just one step in getting you closer to Enlightenment. *Learning to love is the other.* Together they are a powerful force. Throughout this book I've shared lots of ways to help you develop your sixth sense. Here are some ways to help you increase love and bring more light into your life too.

Love Is the Answer

If you want to attract the light to you, you need to signal that you are ready to receive it. You can welcome it by cleaning house. The first things to go should be your fears, as we talked about in chapter 11. Collect them and all the self-limiting beliefs you were taught by early influences in your life—influences that were guided largely by the ego mind. (You will recall that these often include school, religion, and even the unquestioned views your parents and their ancestors held for ages.) Let go of these restrictive beliefs, which no longer serve you, and replace them with your own truths that you have adopted in your life thus far. If you are like me, there are obvious beliefs that never resonated with you, even as a child.

The next step is to make the place cozy. If you are going to be a good home for this light you have to learn to treat yourself with love, respect, and kindness. No matter what you've been told before, you shouldn't feel shame or guilt about caring for yourself first. It's not selfish or ego-driven. In fact, in many cases it's the opposite of that. Think about the safety instructions you're given on airplanes before you fly: parents are always advised to put their own oxygen mask on before assisting their children because they are no good to their kids if they can't breathe. The same logic applies here—if you don't take care of yourself, you can't possibly help others.

You can start by breaking the awful habit of making self-deprecating remarks. Think twice before you say anything negative about your intellect, your body, or your value to family, friends, or society. Speak about yourself in loving terms only. As I've stressed earlier, thoughts are a form of energy. So are words. If you are going to put any energy out there, make sure it works *for* you, not against you.

Take time to pamper yourself. Actions really do speak louder than words. Let your mind, body, and soul all know without question that you value them and are supporting them by meditating, clearing and balancing your chakras (especially the Heart chakra), exercising, eating well, and generally taking good care of your health.

Remind yourself to be open to meeting members of your soul group—this will help attract the people you already chose to support you and your mission in life. They are out there. You will often recognize them by that special comfort you get when they're near—you know, the one that makes you feel as if you've known them for a hundred years even on the first day you meet.

Speak about the members of that group in loving terms too—and extend the same kind of support to them and their mission as you want them to do for you.

Once you've done all of this you are ready to make a soul sacrifice, meaning you are ready to step up and do something that requires effort or commitment for the sake of others in need. Know that as you work for their betterment, you'll also be raising the vibrations of your own soul.

Call on and connect with every celestial source of guidance you have for help. This includes angels of every specialty—joy, communication, concentration, commitment, patience, love, and kindness angels, among others. Reach out to your spirit guides, your teaching guides, and the ascended masters while meditating or praying. Although we have all of these resources available to us at any moment, do not forget that you can always go directly to the ultimate source or God for your strength or power. God is all encompassing, all knowing, and of course, all loving. Again, a simple conversation from your heart will do. And don't forget to consult your own inner soul. It has amassed more knowledge over its lifetimes than you may realize.

Write letters of intent to the Universe. As the Bible tells us, "Ask and you will receive." Composing your thoughts in this way makes the things you hope for clear to yourself as well as to the Creator of all things. Of course, you should be sure to ask that your prayers, wishes, or desires serve the highest good. You don't want it if it takes something away from another person.

Have faith—believe with every fiber of your being that you will be led to the answers and to the fulfillment of your present purpose.

As you drive toward meeting your goals, remember to relinquish control and welcome what the Universe sends you, because it knows best and is sharing that knowledge with you. Keep in mind that if something doesn't come to you after you wait for a while, then it probably wasn't yours to begin with. It wasn't in accordance with the soul contract you signed. You have to let it go. But be assured that what *is* yours will always come to you.

Don't get me wrong. I'm still human too. I get fearful. And there are definitely times when I want what I want. But when the Universe says no, I have to remind myself that God knows what's best for us more than we do, and his time is not always our time. Occasionally the answer will be no. It's not always going to be yes. And that's the whole point. Don't be desperate. Be anxious for nothing because it will come if it's supposed to come, and it will be for everybody's highest good when it does.

A similar patience applies when you get sidetracked from your purpose—when you feel you are floundering because you made a choice that took you off course. In that case, don't get stressed out. Remember that what's happening to you is just one moment in all of eternity—it's a pin dot in time. It's not in the big, big, big picture. The only thing that that left turn can really do is take you down a different path, because your destination was already set. In time you will get where you're meant to be. How long it will take, I don't know. But I do know that whether you take I-95, the freeway, or the side road, you are still going to get to that destination. Don't worry.

Now, with all these recommendations, am I saying your life is going to be perfect?

No. The reason your life won't be perfect is because you will still have to deal with a significant portion of the population that doesn't understand this concept, or maybe has never even heard of it. They have moved so far away from the divine force that they are trying to fill its void with other things, from out-of-control spending, eating, drinking, and smoking to a host of other distractions they hope will give them peace or pleasure. But that doesn't mean you can't be the light wherever you go—one of the ones who illuminates the darkness by simply living in sync with your heart.

I think it's important to say at this point that I will not know all the answers until I myself cross to the other side again or until I finally reach full and complete Enlightenment. As my personal journey, from resisting my gifts to my current understanding of them, proves, we are always learning. But I do trust the sources of what I know so far. I no longer ask, "Why me?" I'm *happy* to be a medium and can see now how much I've benefited from the experience over the years by helping others.

I told you in the introduction that Spirit had a reason for you picking up this book. Yes, learning to understand psychic phenomena, increasing your own intuitive and psychic abilities, or even discovering how to become a medium was part of that reason. But Spirit also really wanted me to encourage you to look more closely at *all* of your gifts, whatever they may be—even if they are well outside the realm of psychic endeavor. Maybe you're a talented computer programmer, musician, chef, designer, detective, nurse, or basketball player. All of our pursuits can be enhanced by a greater connection to light energy. Spirit is okay with us asking "Why me?" about our gifts if we also consider that maybe these strengths exist in us for a purpose—our soul purpose. If you are really into one interest, but feel yourself being pulled toward another the way I was with past-life regressions versus mediumship, don't worry. You may just find a way to use these interests together to do what you do even better.

The subtext of so many of the messages I receive and deliver from the spirit world is that we are not in this life to suffer and sacrifice. Instead, we are here to inspire others by utilizing the gifts from our soul and exercising our unique creativity.

I believe this message is especially important for young people so I will tell you what I tell my own children: It is easy to get caught up in society's expectations of you rather than the expectations you set for yourselves on the other side before you were born. If, however, you look for, identify, and use your best talents for a higher good, you will always find your way. I urge them to also remember that we are all connected to one Source and, therefore, we are never separate from one another. As we pursue and remember our mission, it is also important to forgive others and to love one another unconditionally. Living in love instead of fear, in possibility and light instead of darkness, is how it was meant to be.

In all my years of working with Spirit, I have always asked for the very best messages to be delivered through me. I sincerely hope I delivered the most meaningful messages here too.

My prayer for you is that in each unfolding moment your soul whispers its infinite wisdom into your heart, keeping you forever connected to God's love.

Namaste.

—Kim Russo, the Happy Medium

Author's Note

A Few Words About My Certification

WHEN I WAS IN high school, science was my favorite subject. My sun sign is Gemini, so naturally I love to know how things work. Breaking concepts down into their simplest form is the best way to understand their mechanics, and as you've witnessed in the pages of this book, using that same method is how I figured out how mediumship works for me.

During my many years of being a medium, I've probably met and talked with more dead people than living. I certainly hope I get to meet them again one day when I shed my physical body and return home. I can just imagine it—we'll have one big reunion. When doing a reading, I get to know spirits intimately. It is no different than if I come to your home for dinner and your uncle Bob is sitting next to me at the table. As I talk with him, I become familiar with his many different characteristics: his corny jokes, his infectious laugh, and maybe even his poor table manners. When I meet your relatives during a medium reading, similar aspects of their personalities show themselves. Spirits always come to me in their truest form. I realized a long time ago that if an afterlife didn't exist, I couldn't possibly know all of the obscure details that a spirit shares with me about his life and death during our brief time together. I intuitively knew from a young age that this other world existed, but it was reading after reading that *proved* it to me.

Although I had all of the evidence I needed to convince myself and the myriad people I had read for, I thought it would be amazing to put my abilities to the test. I didn't know where to start at first—there are so few organizations that can vouch for psychic abilities, let alone certify them with a high level of accuracy and credibility. Then I came upon an organization called the Forever Family Foundation. One of their main missions is to provide a forum where individuals and families who have suffered the loss of a loved one can find support, information, and hope through state-of-the-art services backed by ongoing research into the survival of consciousness and afterlife science.

In order to fulfill this important mission, the foundation administers tests to be sure that the mediums listed with their organization have highly developed abilities. I was brought into a large room where I read for several different people on an individual basis. Of course, the foundation selected people with whom I had no prior contact. Then I was scored based on the accuracy of the information I presented to each person I read for.

When I met Bob and Phran, the founders of this nonprofit organization, they instantly felt like kindred souls. Our purposes were aligned and I knew I had found what I was looking for. Although they always show their appreciation to their certified mediums, I'm not sure they know how much we mediums appreciate them in return. They are wonderful people who provide very necessary and valuable resources to those in grief as well as to those of us with mediumistic abilities.

In addition to Bob and Phran, I also appreciate all the other mediums on the team. The organization asks that we donate our time to help the families they serve. As a result, the Forever Family Foundation attracts not only gifted mediums but truly generous mediums as well. All are amazing people with enormous hearts. Collectively we understand how fragile and vulnerable the bereaved can be. Along with the foundation, we all aim to handle every person with nothing but the utmost compassion and love. Not only am I happy to have been one of the original mediums to become certified, along with such other notable mediums as Laura Lynne Jackson, Bobbi Allison, Theresa Caputo, and Doreen Molloy, but I am also proud to sit on the Forever Family Foundation's medium advisory board to better assist them in reaching their goals.

After being a Forever Family Foundation–certified medium for many years, Laura Lynne Jackson—who is a fellow certified medium, the author of *The Light Between Us,* and a very good friend—called me up and suggested that I apply to also become a certified medium with the Windbridge Institute for Applied Research in Human Potential. They too have a marvelous reputation. In fact, she was curious as to why I hadn't already done this. Truth be told, I had briefly thought about applying, but for some reason I was under the impression that I'd have to travel back and forth to Tucson, Arizona, where they are located, to complete the demanding test; I didn't realize that the test could be conducted by phone. Besides, I had overheard two mediums talking at one of the Forever Family Foundation get-togethers about the number of steps it took to become certified with this organization and it sounded very involved. "Really, Laura, you think I would be able to pass?" I said. Laura laughed as she always does when I am being a doubting Thomas and simply said, "Kim, of course I think you'll pass; I did. And besides, your sprit guides are rock stars. They have never, and will never, let you down." Laura always talks sense when I need to hear it, and that talk gave me the encouragement to make the call. She said, "Kim, I think they may only have a couple more spots available to become a certified medium and after that I know they are not taking any more applicants."

The heat was on. I immediately looked at their website to see what I was getting myself into. It's always an intimidating prospect to be tested but especially when there are eight individual steps to the process, including written questionnaires, personality and psychological tests, two phone interviews, two blinded phone readings, mediumship research training, human research subjects training, and lastly, grief training.

I loved that the cofounders, Dr. Julie Beischel and Mark Boccuzzi, and their team had such a compelling mission statement. It reads, and I quote, "Launched in 2008, the Windbridge Institute, LLC, is dedicated to conducting world-class research on phenomena currently unexplained within traditional scientific disciplines. Our primary focus is on applied research with the goal of developing and distributing information, services, and technologies that allow people to reach their full potential so they can live happier, healthier, and more fulfilling lives."

I liked the vibe I was getting all the way around, especially since I love scientific research and they are an independent research organization consisting of a community of scientists with varied backgrounds, specialties, and interests. "What do I have to lose?" I thought. I always love a challenge, so I picked up the phone and spoke to Julie. She was really cool and I could sense her passion for the research was matched only by her sharp scientific mind. She was very up-front and explained everything that would be required of me. What read like a long laundry list on the site now sounded like a super-exciting challenge. I was totally into it. I couldn't wait to undergo all of the steps to see if my abilities would prevail.

I remember each step being nerve-racking in its own way. In addition to a lengthy interview with a member of the administration to determine more about my personality, intentions, and ethics, I had an in-depth peer interview with a previously certified medium. But the step that sticks out in my mind more than all the others was one of the blind readings. I was told I'd receive a call from someone who would remain completely anonymous. There would be no indication if the caller was a man or a woman. When the phone rang and I answered, I was to wait until the caller pressed a number on a keypad. The tone that followed was my signal that someone was indeed on the line. Although I was supposed to channel a deceased person, I was given no idea if that deceased person belonged to the caller or to someone else. I didn't even know if what I was relaying made any sense to the listener or not. The only thing I was completely sure of was what I was seeing, hearing, and feeling. At this point, all I could do was trust the information Spirit was providing. While I was channeling, I heard nothing from the caller—not even a throat clearing, an "uh-huh," or a peep of any kind. It was just me and the deceased doing our thing. Once again I had to have complete faith in the other side to bring it, and bring it they *did*.

A few months after completing the rigorous testing, I received the good news that I was officially a certified medium with the Windbridge Institute. I currently volunteer my time for both of these wonderful organizations, and as sure as I know my name is Kim Russo, I also know our soul survives physical death. I remain optimistic that science will someday prove it beyond all doubt.

Acknowledgments

To MY EARTHLY FATHER: You are the best dad a girl could have ever asked for. When I am having a rough day, the memory of your bright smile and your infectious laugh makes it all better. It is you who taught me the true meaning of hard work and who directed me not to follow my dreams but to chase them. Well, Dad, chase them I did, and I hope you are proud of me. Rest in peace and continue to fly with the angels. I miss you more than words can say but I've learned it's never good-bye—it's till we meet again . . . PS: I love you more . . .

To my mother who has always believed in me and never once questioned my abilities even when I did: Thank you for giving me a solid foundation and for teaching me to have faith by trusting that I am always right where I am supposed to be and to *never* sweat the small stuff. Mom, you taught me that my voice does matter in this world and to trust my intuition at all times. But most of all, thank you for teaching me how important it is to always listen to my heart.

To my husband, Anthony, who had me at "Hello": I thank God every day for bringing me a man as wonderful as you and I appreciate you in every way. Your unconditional love and endless sacrifices make it possible for me to share my gift with the world. It is by example that you taught me how to be a better version of myself, and there is no one else I'd rather share this amazing adventure with than you. I love you, Boo!

To my children, Nicholas, Joseph, and Anthony Jr.: Thank you for picking me to be your mom. Not only did you satisfy my soul's desire to experience unconditional love, but because of you, all of my expectations of being a mom have been exceeded. You guys have made my life complete and I can't wait to see the wonderful contributions your souls will make to this world in the future. I love you to infinity and beyond!

To my sister, Susan: Thank you for always being there for me and for your unwavering support and protection, especially as a child during my long, dark, sleepless nights. You have done things for me that only a sister would do, like pretending you were me and calling my boss to quit my job. Shhh . . . I'll never tell. I love that we don't need words to communicate and that you always know what I'm thinking; for example, a simple kick under the table or an eye roll says it all. As the saying goes, "Blood makes us family, but our hearts make us friends."

To my brother, Neil: Thank you for being you. I love all of our long, deep conversations about life. Thank you for always keeping it real and most of all, thank you for always making me laugh; you are the funniest person I know. Although Dad left some *big* shoes to fill, you definitely fit the bill. I love you so much.

To my sister-in-law, Theresa, and my brother-in-law, Jack, who left us way too soon: Thank you for continuing to watch over our family and for consistently letting us feel your presence. There are no words to describe the impact you've had on our lives. The world is a better place because you were born.

To my cousins, Mary Randazzo and Carmela Mosti: You girls are not only my cousins; you are also my childhood playmates and forever friends. Thank you for always being there for me and for all of your love and support throughout the years. I am so lucky to have you in my life. They say you can't pick your family but, given the choice, I would pick you girls over and over.

To all of my soul sisters, Camille Marra Merollo, Bobbi Allison, Laura Lynne Jackson, Stephanie Rose Vriniotis, Maria Matera, Dorene Bair, Pat Longo, and Lisa Austin, just to name a few (everyone else, you know who you are): I thank God every day for giving me girlfriends whom I admire and respect, with whom I can laugh and cry. But most of all, with whom I can just be *me*. In your own unique ways, you have all added a piece of magic to my life.

To everyone who believed in me: I call you my teacher. Each and every one of you has made a difference in my life at the perfect time. Thank you for appearing when the student was ready. Especially to Holly Chalnick. Thank you for never giving up on me and for always encouraging me to stay on course. Not only did I have you to guide me here on earth, but I am forever grateful that you are still guiding me from the afterlife. You have truly paid it forward, and I know that like an angel, you've earned your wings.

To Barry Rosenberg and Linda Stasi: Thank you for recognizing that I have something special and for going the distance on my behalf. I will be forever grateful.

To all of my students of the Enchanted Circle: Thank you for trusting me to help you develop your precious gifts. The energetic bonds that were created during our time together shall be forever embedded in time and space and forever in our hearts. Although you call me teacher, I continue to learn something valuable from each of you. May your lights continue to shine ever so brightly for the world to see.

Thank you to all of the people at LMN for believing in me and for giving me a universal platform to allow me to help raise the consciousness of humanity.

To my collaborator Hope Innelli: Thank you for your countless hours and tireless efforts to make sure every page in this book was perfectly written. Because of your sharp attention to detail and dedication to this project, the words in this book have come to life—and like a well-orchestrated piece of music, so has this become music for our souls.

To my publishing guides Lisa Sharkey, Claudia Riemer Boutote, and Amy Bendell: Thank you for believing in me and for giving me a voice through the power of this book. And thanks to Suzanne Wickham, Jennifer Jenson, Alieza Schvimer, Alyssa Rueben, Dave Roberge, and Max Gettinger for all your contributions to the process.

To all of my fans and to the readers who are holding this book at this very moment: Thank you for allowing me to share my story with you. I told you there was a reason you picked up this book and I hope you found many as you went along. Whether the reason was contained in one chapter, one paragraph, or even in one word, I thank and applaud you for taking the first step to discovering your true identity. Remember, "We are not human beings having a spiritual experience, but rather, we are spiritual beings having a human experience."

Namaste.

—Kim Russo